D1104954

ENGLISH ADVENTURERS AND EMIGRANTS, 1609 – 1660

ENGLISH ADVENTURERS AND EMIGRANTS, 1609 – 1660

Abstracts of Examinations in the High Court
of Admiralty with Reference to Colonial America

Peter Wilson Coldham

GENEALOGICAL PUBLISHING CO., INC.
Baltimore 1984

Published by Genealogical Publishing Co., Inc.
Baltimore, Maryland, 1984
Copyright © 1984 by
Peter Wilson Coldham
Surrey, England
All Rights Reserved
Library of Congress Catalogue Card Number 84-80790
International Standard Book Number 0-8063-1082-0
Made in the United States of America

CONTENTS

INTRODUCTION

The High Court of Admiralty (HCA) can trace its history back to the reign of Edward III (1327-1377) when it acquired jurisdiction over cases involving piracy on the high seas. Until the 16th century trials for piratical activities continued to be its main stock in trade but from about 1625, when the Duke of Richmond was patented as Lord High Admiral of England, it assimilated from Chancery almost all civil and criminal cases affecting ships and merchandise at sea, on navigable waterways and over the seas. Records of this court survive from the time of Henry VIII (1509-1547) and, by their very nature, have much to tell us about the early colonizing activities of the New England, Plymouth, Newfoundland, Canada, Virginia and other London Companies as well as the entrepreneurial ventures of private companies and individuals involved in assisting trade and emigration to the new plantations.

Until now little attempt appears to have been made to harness the rich resources of the HCA in any considered way for the benefit of the historian or genealogist, though with one notable exception. This was High Court of Admiralty Examinations 1637-1638 by Dorothy O. Shilton and Richard Holworthy published in 1932 by the Anglo-American Records Foundation Ltd. to which I am indebted for having provided the first inspiration to compile the present work.

To bring within the compass of a single volume a profusion of people, events and opinions chronicled in HCA records as having been concerned in the early foundations of colonial America has required the exercise of a degree of editorial discretion which has of necessity been arbitrary though hopefully falling short of idiosyncracy. Thus the Examination Books have been selected as the prime source of information since they appear to offer the most detailed and balanced accounts of events. The reader will, however, understand that the abstracts in this volume are highly condensed versions of the original entries and aim to provide the textual and chronological context to facilitate reference to other case papers in the HCA collections.

Up to the end of the first quarter of the 17th century most cases involving the Americas have been noticed but thereafter, with only rare exceptions, the abstracts have concentrated upon the mainland territories to the exclusion of Canada, Newfoundland and the West Indian islands. Other major excisions have borne heavily upon lawyers' ramblings and repetitions, merchants' accounts and balance sheets, navigational treatises and archaic circumlocutions. An apology is due to those who have a taste for the language and syntax of the age of Raleigh, Milton and Pepys, since this volume is presented in an idiom calculated to be readily comprehensible to our own age.

Sources

The following classes of records have been used as the basis of this book:

Examinations in Equity Causes. (HCA 13/39-73).

These are large volumes, each covering roughly a two year span and containing fair copies of depositions made in London in support of the allegations of plaintiffs and defendants (and often both). Except between 1651 and 1660 the personal details of each examinant (deponent) were written in a Latin formulary though the matter of the depositions mercifully appears in English. Since entries were made on a day-to-day basis the depositions relevant to any one case tend to appear like scatter-shot throughout a volume, though usually with a marginal identification of the case concerned. The dates shown in this book immediately following the title of the suit are those on or between which relevant depositions will be found.

Examinations by Commission. (HCA 13/226ff.).

These constitute a separate series within the class HCA 13 and are depositions taken outside London, usually at one of the major ports and usually relating to ships registered there. Each set of depositions was written on parchment and returned to the HCA in a roll, in which form they have been preserved.

Examinations in Criminal Cases. (HCA 1/47-50).

This series, similar in form and content to the Equity Examination Books, though considerably less voluminous, has been quarried up to the year 1653 when the sequence is interrupted until 1674.

Interrogatories. (HCA 23).

These set out the questions to be asked of witnesses and, because of the close detail in which deponents were usually interrogated, the substance of each case emerges clearly. This series was examined for those periods for which Equity Examination Books have been withdrawn as unfit, i.e. 1610-1620, 1625-1629 and 1645-1647.

Associated Documents

The following classes of HCA documents are likely to prove helpful in completing a comprehensive study of any one of the cases mentioned in this volume:

Libels. (HCA 24).

Original Bills of Complaint, allegations and exhibits will be found in this class.

Answers. (HCA 13/100ff.).

Replies by defendants to Bills of Complaint.

Indictments and Proceedings. (HCA 1/1-27).

Peter Wilson Coldham
Purley, Surrey,   Lent 1984
England.   AMDG

VOLUME 39

LAURENCE MELATIM/MILITIM v RICHARD HALL (also HALL v MILITIM). 1 June 1608 to 21 June 1609.

John Webb of the City of London, where he was born, merchant aged 23. He provided goods which were delivered on board the Ulysses, owned by Mr. Richard Hall, merchant of London, to be shipped to the West Indies to the account of Tiberio Scievoli and there to be transferred to the St. Mary. The purser of the Ulysses was Thomas Goddard.

Marino Gandini, servant of Laurence Militim with whom he has lived for eight years, but born at Ragusa, aged 28. He was on the Ulysses and saw goods received by Scievoli for the use of Michael Surgo and Paul Pieres, merchants of Ragusa, for the St. Mary, but before they could be delivered to her the Spaniards had seized the ship and the goods were sold instead to the Spaniards and to the Indians they kept to kill cows and make hides. In the West Indies a hundred of bread was worth seven or eight hides.

Thomas Goddard of the City of London, where he has lived for eight years, merchant aged 28. Richard Hall owned the Ulysses of London and fitted her out for a trading voyage to the West Indies under John Lock as Master and the deponent as purser. (Vol. 40).

Robert Sharpe of the City of London, where he has lived for 12 years, merchant aged 32. Militim put one Maryne in charge of the provisions destined for the St. Mary but, when the Ulysses arrived at Pointe Ray in the West Indies, he sold them instead of bartering them for pearls and tobacco as had been intended. The bread was then found to be mouldy and the pork and cheese spent. (Vol. 40).

ENGLISH ADVENTURERS

SIR FRANCIS POPHAM AND LADY ANNE POPHAM, WIDOW, v JOHN HAVERCOMBE. 10 to 18 June 1608. **DON ALPHONSO DE VELASCO, LEGATE OF SPAIN,** v RICHARD HALL. 17 to 26 November 1610. (Vol. 41).

Lancelot Booker of the City of London, where he has lived for 15 years, but born at Rotherham, Yorkshire, aged 33. He was homeward bound from the West Indies on the Penelope of London belonging to Richard Hall when, on 5 July 1607, they encountered the Gift of God, Master John Havercombe and Captain George Popham, 60 leagues from the Isle of Flowers bound for Virginia. The deponent was transferred to the Gift of God to be her cooper and went with her to the north parts of Virginia where they arrived in August 1607. There George Popham took up his appointment as President of the Council in the newly built town called St. George. Other Members of the Council included Rawleigh Gilbert, Gawyn Cury, Robert Seaman, James Davies, Edward Harley and John Elliott.

In October 1607 Popham determined to send the Gift of God back to England in consort with the Mary and John but then received intelligence from the savages of those parts that the French were coming to besiege them. He therefore ordered Havercombe to remain with his ship in the harbour of Sakudahoc to guard the settlement and she was detained there for eight or nine weeks. When the Gift of God finally sailed for England in December 1607 John Elliott was appointed as her Captain and Popham instructed him in writing to make for the Azores for victuals and repairs. Such was the shortage of food and drink on board that one of the ship's company died before reaching the Azores and two more before she reached England. In the Azores 33 masts and a cable were sold from the ship and one of her guns was pawned.

ENGLISH ADVENTURERS

John Deaman of Stoke Gabriel, Devon, sailor aged 55. He was hired by Sir John Popham deceased to go as quartermaster of the Gift of God and sailed from Plymouth for Virginia in May or June 1607.

Timothy Savidge of St. Katherine's precincts where and at Horsey Down he has lived for three years, but born at St. Bride's, London, sailor aged 55. Sir John Popham, late Lord Chief Justice of England, hired him as a quartermaster. In the extremity of frost at Sakudahoc a plank in the Gift of God was broken and water rushed in the ship. She arrived at Holford, Cornwall, in February 1607/8 having left Virginia on 15 December.

John Fletcher of Limehouse, Middlesex, sailor aged 27, served as a common man on the Gift of God.

John Elliott of Newland Fee, Essex, aged 24. He was appointed to go to Virginia by Lord Chief Justice Popham who was an adventurer there with Sir Ferdinando Gorges, Sir Francis Popham and Sir Bartholomew Michell.

Augustine Phillips of the City of London, barber surgeon aged 23. He was engaged as surgeon of the Penelope for a trading voyage to Hispaniola. When she arrived at Cape St. Anthony she was attacked and fired upon by an unidentified vessel of 300 tons. In the ensuing fight the Penelope gained the upper hand and took the foreign ship back to Plymouth. Despite the amity between England and Spain, many English vessels had been attacked and taken by the Spanish in the West Indies. At Cape Tiberoone the Penelope loaded 3000 hides. (Vol. 41).

Israell Dale of Rochester, Kent, gunner aged 30. The Penelope sailed from London in July 1608 and the deponent was hired by her Master, William Warner. (Vol. 41).

ENGLISH ADVENTURERS

Lucas Pinchback of Ratcliffe, Middlesex, where he has lived for 10 years, shipwright aged 30. The Penelope was loaded in London with silks, silk stockings, linen cloth and other goods to be trucked in the West Indies. The ship which attacked her was manned by Spaniards, Portuguese, Flemings and some negroes and was found to be laden with hides and tallow. (Vol. 41).

Peter Cannon of Ratcliffe, Middlesex, where he has lived for 10 years, sailor aged 23. He was boatswain of the Penelope. (Vol. 41).

William Warner of the City of London, sailor aged 35. (Vol. 41).

Richard Bracey of Ratcliffe, Middlesex, where he has lived for 16 years, sailor aged 34. He was Master's Mate of the Penelope, a vessel of 100 tons. When the Spaniards came aboard his ship in Trinidad they sought to betray her by persuading her company to sail to Cape Tres Puntos where they promised they would bring pearls but meanwhile sent soldiers there to capture her. But the ship got away and traded at Cape Tiberoone. (Vol. 41).

VOLUME 40

ALICE SIDDALL v JOHN ELDRED and RICHARD HALL. 5 May 1609 to 5 June 1610.

Thomas Mun of London, where he was born, merchant aged 27. Eldred and Hall were owners of the Mayflower which in 1603 was fitted out for a voyage to the West Indies and in 1605 arrived at Leghorn where the deponent then was. William Siddall and William Resold were on the voyage, the latter as factor for the owners. At Leghorn the ship was impressed into the Great Duke's service and her company were banished.

James Woodcott of Ratcliffe, Middlesex, where he was born, sailor aged 23. He piloted the ship to the Downs on her outward voyage when her Master was Andrew Miller and William Resold was one of the company.

Andrew Milner/Miller of the City of London, where he has lived for 10 years, sailor aged 44. He was Master of the ship and employed William Siddall as Master of a pinnace in the West Indies. Siddall received pay at Leghorn.

Lucas Pinchback (again) of Wapping, Middlesex, where he has lived for 16 years, aged 27. He went as a carpenter in the Mayflower.

John Moulde of Ratcliffe, Middlesex, where he has lived 12 years, sailor aged 45. Siddall served in the ship as a midshipman.

William Resold of London, where he has lived for 34 years, merchant aged 50. (Vols. 40 & 41).

Henry Robinson of London, where he was born, merchant aged 28. He was Eldred's factor at Leghorn where the Mayflower was recaulked on her arrival. She was due to go from there to London. (Vol. 41).

Jonas Verdon, servant of John Eldred with whom he has lived for 8 years, aged 24. Andrew Miller was given money by Eldred with which to pay wages before the ship left London in December 1602, and was given further money on his return to London. (Vol. 41).

George Smith of the City of London, scrivener aged 35. In February 1605/6 Andrew Miller signed a deed releasing Eldred and Hall from all actions he had against them.

VOLUME 43

WILLIAM WYE v. THOMAS SHEPPARD: VIRGINIA COMPANY v. WILLIAM WYE. 15 April 1620 to 8 May 1622.

ENGLISH ADVENTURERS

Summary. In June 1619 the Garland, Mr. William Wye, sailed from London chartered to Thomas Sheppard and John Farrer to carry goods and passengers to the Somers Islands (Bermuda) and Virginia, including some passengers who had been transferred from the Bona Nova which had left London for Virginia earlier but was disabled and returned to port. In October 1619 the Garland arrived off Gurnard's Head, Bermuda, but was overtaken by a great tempest, driven against the rocks, dismasted and nearly wrecked. Her passengers and cargo were put ashore with difficulty and Wye arranged with the Governor to refit the ship using materials from the Warwick which had previously foundered in Bermuda. Wye then decided not to continue his voyage to James Town, Virginia, but to return to England taking with him the tobaccos originally intended to have been shipped in the Warwick. He arrived back in London in March 1620.

Richard Daye of Ratcliffe, Middlesex, sailor aged 41. The owners of the Garland were William Wye and Christopher Whitlocke & Co. The deponent witnessed the ship's arrival at Gurnard's Head and learned that many of her company had fallen sick on the voyage from London when victuals ran short. Before he returned to England, Wye made arrangements for those of his passengers who were intended for Virginia to be carried there.

John Daye of Harwich, Essex, native and resident of that place, sailor aged 40.

Thomas Hopkins of Redrith, Surrey, sailor aged 43. He was mate of the Garland. (2 examinations).

Thomas Foster of Giggleswick in Craven, Yorkshire, gent aged 32, deposes about the arrival in Bermuda of the Garland in which he sent back tobaccos to London.

Richard Middleton of Langwith, Westmorland, where he was raised and has lived, gent aged 28. He was part owner of tobaccos brought home on the Garland.

ENGLISH ADVENTURERS

Thomas Claisye of Limehouse, Middlesex, sailor aged 40.

Alexander Farr of St. Olave, Southwark, Surrey, sailor aged 24. He lives by going to sea. Two of the passengers left in Bermuda were sent on Wye's account as well as one seaman who asked to be left there.

Jeremias Keningham of Horsley Down, Surrey, sailor aged 29.

William Wye of Limehouse, Middlesex, surgeon aged 25. He lives by going to sea as a surgeon.

John Johnson of Limehouse, Middlesex, sailor. (2 depositions). He went as pilot of the Garland. Wye caused some passengers to be hung up by the arms and legs, including one named (Henry) Reade, until they confessed to thieving.

John Cuff, citizen of London, merchant aged 39. He went out as Cape Merchant in the Warwick and returned in the Garland. When he shipped passengers on his own account at Gravesend in the Garland to be sent to Virginia there were then aboard some 200 men, women and children of which 40 were intended for Virginia.

Richard Wiseman, citizen of London aged 31. At the beginning of April 1619 he sent goods and passengers to Bermuda in the Gilliflower of London, Mr. William Craforthe, and in June 1619 in the Seaflower of London, Mr. Edward Gardiner. Both ships had helped carry ashore passengers from the Garland. The deponent was never in Bermuda.

William Besse of the Somers Islands where he has lived more than 6 years, yeoman aged 35. (A second deposition describes him as of St. Mildred Poultry, London, girdler aged 35). Ships have been coming to Bermuda and unloading there for the past 9 years since the islands began to be planted and inhabited. He came home on the Garland.

ENGLISH ADVENTURERS

William Ewens of Limehouse, Middlesex, sailor aged 40. He went 5 or 6 years ago to Bermuda in the <u>George</u> of London with passengers and goods and it was customary for ships to land them there.

John Hudlestone of Ratcliffe, Middlesex, sailor aged 33. About 10 years ago he was quartermaster of the <u>Starre</u> of London which took passengers and goods to Bermuda, and 4 years ago went as mate of the same ship. In 1619 he went as Master of the <u>Bona Nova</u> intended for Virginia and returned to Ratcliffe. Bermuda having newly begun to be inhabited, the people there have no means, nor will they carry passengers and goods ashore.

Francis Mosse, citizen of London aged 49. He was a signatory to the charter party for the <u>Garland</u> but did not embark on her.

Thomas Melling of the City of London, merchant aged 38, owner of land in Bermuda and Member of the Virginia Company. He had people in Bermuda and every year for several years has contracted with Mr. Chamberlain, merchant of London, who also has people there, to send goods and provisions to the islands. By the <u>Garland</u> he sent goods to Mr. Seymour in Bermuda.

William Webb of the City of London, merchant aged 55 and husband for 7 years of the Virginia Company who freighted 103 of its members in the <u>Garland</u>.

Edward Collingwood gent, citizen of London. Adventurers of the Virginia Company pay £12.10s. for a single share entitling them to 100 acres of land in Virginia.

Francis Carter, citizen of London, barber surgeon aged 54. In June 1618 an order was made by the Virginia Company that every person transported to Virginia should be assured of 100 acres of land.

John Bland, citizen of London, merchant aged 49. He has seen letters written by the Governor of Bermuda and by Ferdinando Sheppard about the <u>Garland</u>'s voyage.

ENGLISH ADVENTURERS

Richard Bull, citizen of London, fishmonger aged 28, deposes as to the extent of losses incurred by the Virginia Company.

Richard Caswell, citizen of London, baker aged ?43. He has shares in the Virginia Company.

Ferdinando Sheppard of Rollright, Oxfordshire, gent aged 22, brother of Thomas Sheppard and brother-in-law of John Farrer. He was orioginally a passenger on the Bona Nova but transferred to the Garland on which there were 130 passengers of whom 40, mostly carpenters, sawyers and bricklayers, were destined for Virginia. On passage the ship's carpenter, the cooper, and two of the company died and many others were taken sick. Henry Reade drew his sword against Captain Wye who threatened to duck him.

Robert Fowler of Tower Precinct, London, gent aged 19, another passenger in the Bona Nova who transferred to the Garland, deposes about landing places in Bermuda.

Thomas Downam of ?Combe Hay, Somerset, gent aged 27, examined as to events in Bermuda. (Vol. 44).

John Havard, inhabitant of the Somer Islands aged 52, examined as to events there. (Vol. 44).

Anthony Grove, citizen of London, gent aged 31, examined as to events in Bermuda. (Vol. 44).

John Smith of Ratcliffe, Middlesex, cooper aged 28, examined as to events in Bermuda. (Vol. 44).

Nicholas Farrer of the City of London, gent aged 27, brother of John Farrer (3 examinations). The Virginia Company provisioned the Garland for 44 persons to be shipped to Virginia of whom 39 went by that ship and 5 were left out to be shipped later. One named Pritchard and a boy were shipped to Virginia at Sheppard's and Farrer's expense.

ENGLISH ADVENTURERS

The Company also paid for one Clarke and 4 others to go in the <u>Warwick</u> to Bermuda and Virginia. Those men who were appointed to go to Virginia but who were stranded in Bermuda were sent on purpose to build houses and to make provision for a further supply of men to set up an iron works; those shipped on the <u>Garland</u> were of extraordinary quality, fit for the erection of an iron works, mills and other "commodities" suitable to that country. The Company had entrusted to Wye, Captain Whitney and Ferdinando Sheppard letters to Governor Yardley of Virginia which were to be carried in the <u>Garland</u>. It had been agreed that each person shipped to Virginia before Midsummer 1625, if he continued there for 3 years or should die there, would be entitled to 100 acres of land, 50 acres on the first division and another 50 afterwards, without paying rent to the Company. For want of instructions from the Company, Governor Yardley had not known how to proceed with the Chickahominie Indians to punish them for the great cruelties they had inflicted upon the English nation.

Humphrey Sherbrooke of Horsley Down, Surrey, sailor aged 47. He was one of the company of the <u>Bona Nova</u>.

Nicholas Buckeridge, citizen of London, grocer aged 40. (2 examinations). He had helped examine Sheppard's and Farrer's account books to identify charges for passengers Pittman and Clerke and others destined for Bermuda, for 39 passengers intended for Virginia, and for 9 others destined for Virginia by ships other than the <u>Garland</u>, the greater part of whose passengers had first been shipped in the <u>Bona Nova</u>.

John Duncon of Poplar, Middlesex, sailor aged 36. (3 examinations). He was one of the company of the <u>Bona Nova</u> who transferred to the <u>Garland</u>. Henry Reade had made a written complaint against Wye for threatening to duck him.

Thomas Hopkins of Redrith, Surrey, sailor aged 42.

ENGLISH ADVENTURERS

William Eden of Limehouse, Middlesex, sailor aged 24. When the Garland arrived at Bermuda there were no more than 14 or 15 healthy seamen in her.

ROWLAND GOLDE v. JOHN BURFITT. 13 May & 22 June 1621.

Richard Page of St. Katherine's, London, sailor aged 26. Rowland Golde was part owner of the Falcon, Mr. Thomas Jones, which was chartered for James Town, Virginia, Newfoundland, Malaga and home. John Burfitt, John Merritt, John Waltham, Edward Smith, Richard Browne, Thomas Hasteles, William Humfrey and others made up her company. When she arrived in Virginia, Thomas Jones covenanted with William Tucker, William Capps, William Gayne, William Gauntlett and Thomas Brewood of Kicotan to take sassafras from them direct to London.

William Kinge of Blackwall, Middlesex, sailor aged 26.

UNNAMED SUIT. 15 September 1621.

Richard Hooper of Wapping, Middlesex, sailor, examined for Francis and Thomas Challoner, creditors of David Middleton. When the Jonathan of London was in the Downs in March 1619/20 bound for Virginia, David Middleton shipped two persons called Lewknor and Arthur Middleton for that place. On passage David Middleton, a corpulent great man, full faced and full of grey hairs, died. Arthur Middleton always called him father.

Edward Bassocke of Wapping, Middlesex, late purser of the Jonathan deposes similarly.

VOLUME 44

ARNOLD GARDNER v. ----- GATES. 19 October & 28 November 1622.

ENGLISH ADVENTURERS

William Forward of Limehouse, Middlesex, aged 35, examined for Edward Bennett of London, merchant. (2 examinations). He was the gunner of the Seaflower, Mr. Edmund Gardiner, which developed a leak on her way to Virginia and was diverted to Nevis. The Warwick, which had left the Downs only 5 days before her, arrived in Virginia 6 weeks before her. While the Seaflower was riding at Kika--han, about two miles from the town, her Master sent Gates, who had come as a passenger to Virginia, to fetch tobaccos aboard belonging to the said Gates and to Maurice Thompson.

George Page of Wapping, Middlesex, mariner, was boatswain of the Seaflower and considered her unfit for the voyage. She remained in Virginia for 6 weeks.

ROBERT, EARL OF WARWICK v. EDWARD BREWSTER. 29 January 1622/3 to 4 June 1624. (A full account of the events described appears in Virginia Magazine Vol. 87 No. 1. - January 1979).

Edward Withers of St. Katherine's Precinct, London, gent aged 25. By agreement with Warwick, Sir Samuel Argall had prepared a storehouse in Virginia to contain provisions for the ship Treasurer to enable her to make a fishing voyage to Newfoundland. While making her way to James City in 1618 the Treasurer, Mr. Daniel Elfrey, was overtaken by the Neptune of London, Mr. Edward Bruster, who then took command of both ships, the Neptune being of greater burden and strength. The deponent was an attendant of Lord Delaware and a passenger in the Neptune. When both ships were 400 leagues from James City, Bruster ordered men and provisions to be taken from the Neptune and put on the Treasurer which, on their arrival in Virginia, were handed over to Captain Argall. For that reason the Treasurer was rendered unable to undertake her intended fishing voyage.

John Martyn of London, gent aged 29, born "in America in Persia" and christened in his own country and can say the Apostles' Creed and the Lord's Prayer. He was a passenger to Virginia in the Neptune as an attendant on Lord Delaware. The Earl of Warwick was generally reputed to be the owner of the Treasurer and to have fitted her out for her voyage to James Town. Captain Argall sent the ship to Bermuda to obtain victuals and on the way she met an empty Angola ship from which she took 25 negroes before completing her voyage and returning to Virginia.

Augustine Steward of St. Leonard, Shoreditch, London, gent aged 38. He was a passenger in the Neptune.

John Drason of Greenwich, Kent, sailor aged 44.

Richard Beamont of Ratcliffe, Middlesex, sailor aged 43.

John Wood of Wapping, Middlesex, sailor aged 50. After the Treasurer returned from Bermuda to Virginia she was taken into a creek where she overturned and was sunk. Her company went ashore to live.

John Pettie (Petty) of Walthamstow, Essex, barber surgeon.

Richard Pulley of Staple Inn, London, aged 32, examined as to Chancery proceedings in Argall v. Bruster in Easter Term 1623.

Rowland Mather of St. Clement Danes, Westminster, gent aged 43, also examined as to Chancery proceedings.

Henry Ibbutson of Isleworth, Middlesex, gent aged 19. He is a young man who does not know what his friends will leave him but is already of settled worth and comes to depose at Bruster's request. The Neptune sighted the Treasurer in June 1618 off the St. Michael's Islands. Martyn, Argall's Persian-born servant, fell out with Edward Bruster over Lord Delaware's goods and is still malicious about the subject.

ENGLISH ADVENTURERS

Henry Tawny of Wingham (?Winchcombe) in the county of Gloucester, barber surgeon aged 29, is not in debt and comes to depose at Lady Delaware's request. He has no skill in navigation. Eleven men only were taken from the Neptune and put on the Treasurer.

Edward Constable of St. Clement Danes, Westminster, scissor maker aged 47. He is worth £30 and took passage in the Treasurer which Warwick had declared he was consigning to his cousin Captain Argall.

Sibell, wife of Edward Constable (above), aged 36. She went with her husband in the Treasurer to Virginia.

Thomas Hopkins of Redriffe, Surrey, sailor aged 46.

Thomas Smith is produced as a witness at the request of Lady Delaware.

William Blackwell of Grays near Henley, Oxfordshire, gent aged 51.

RE THOMAS HAMOR. 11 & 19 June 1623.

Samuel Moll of Rochelle, France, but having come from Virginia, surgeon aged 41, examined on behalf of Hester Hamor. In January 1622/3 a coffin was made at James Town, Virginia, by Nathaniel Jeffryes, a joiner dwelling there, to bury the corpse of Thomas Hamor who had died there.

Dennis Davys of St. Giles, Cripplegate, London, barber surgeon aged 35. He was well acquainted with Hamor who died in James City and was at his burial.

Thomas Edwards of St. Mary Aldermary, London, salter aged 34. He was in Virginia as purser of the Abigall of London and witnessed the burial of Hamor whom he knew.

ENGLISH ADVENTURERS

RE THE PARAGON. 12 July & 17 November 1623.

Thomas Hewes of London, mariner. He was Master of the Paragon which was struck by a great storm on 8 February 1622/3 near the Western Isles while on a voyage from London to New England. Her boat was put overboard and was lost while the ship suffered damage and much of her cargo was washed overboard.

Augustine Breight of Deptford, Kent, shipwright. He was carpenter of the Paragon.

William Peirse of Ratcliffe, Middlesex, mariner aged 32, examined about the extent of damage to the Paragon.

EDMUND BARKER & ----- VEGA v. NATHANIEL BUTLER. 29 September 1624 to 9 February 1624/5.

Edward Soame of Limehouse, Middlesex, sailor aged 31. The James, Mr. Nathaniel Butler, owned by Edmund Barker & Co., was chartered for Bermuda two years ago and returned to London with tobacco and a number of Spaniards who had been freighted at £5 a head.

John Hill of St. Anne, Blackfriars, London, gent aged 38, servant of Nathaniel Butler. Soon after the James arrived back in London, James Butler, natural brother of Nathaniel Butler, demanded that the tobacco on board be delivered to him.

James Butler of Tedingham, Essex, merchant aged 38.

Henry Tawny of Winchcombe, Gloucestershire, barber surgeon aged 31.

Robert Davenport of Wandsworth, Surrey, gent aged 29. He went to Bermuda two years ago and stayed there for 10 weeks during which time he heard that the Spanish ship St. Anthony had run ashore there a year previously with a cargo of tobacco, gold ingots and jewels.

ENGLISH ADVENTURERS

Captain Butler, who was then Governor there, had the Spaniards brought before him and arranged for them and the tobacco to be transported in two English ships to England. The deponent returned to England in the <u>Marathon</u> two years ago.

HENRY STARKY v. JACOB BANCKES.
16 October 1624.

Robert Cole of Dover, Kent, barber surgeon aged 29. He was surgeon of the <u>Silver Falcon</u> of which John Fermer was Captain, Henry Bacon Master and Henry Starky Master's Mate. She went to the West Indies to load tobacco and carried it to Flushing where it was received by Jacob Banckes. Edward, Lord Zouch, was an adventurer in the ship.

WILLIAM STEVENS & THOMAS FELL v THE LITTLE JAMES. 17 to 20 November 1624.

Edward Winslow of Plymouth, New England, yeoman aged 30, on behalf of the Treasurer and Society of Plymouth Merchants in which he has adventured £60. When the <u>Little James</u> arrived in New England her Captain, Emanuel Altham, and her Master, John Bridges, complained to Governor William Bradford that William Stevens and Thomas Fell had behaved badly on the voyage and sought the Governor's authority for their discharge. The ship sank at Pemaquid in New England for want of a good mooring and her provisions and powder were spoiled. She was righted and repaired by her company and the people of Plymouth. The deponent has been a member of the Plymouth Company since its foundation during which time William Bradford and Isaac Allerton have been Governors.

William Peirce/Peirse of Ratcliffe, Middlesex, sailor aged 33. He has adventured £20 in the Plymouth Company and believes that the sinking of the ship was occasioned by the disorderly conduct of Stevens and Fell.

ENGLISH ADVENTURERS

Because of the accident the Little James was unable to complete her proposed fishing voyage and took little fish home to England where it was found to be unmerchantable.

Bennet Morgan of Plymouth, New England, sailor aged 27. When the Little James arrived in New England her company refused to go on a fishing voyage unless they received their wages, and the examinant believes she was bulged and sunk by the extremity of the weather and not by any fault of her company, though Stevens and Fell forsook the ship and took no pains for her recovery.

Robert Cushman of Rosemary Lane, London, yeoman aged 45. He has been a member of the Plymouth Company for 4 years and was present when the charter party for the Little James was drawn up. The Company's Treasurer, James Sherley, persuaded Stevens and Fell to go the New England as planters for shares and not for wages. They agreed to serve the Plymouth Company in the ship and afterwards in the plantation. As an adventurer in the Plymouth Company the deponent witnessed the agreement made with Stevens and Fell.

James Sherley, citizen of London aged 33. When he was Treasurer of the Plymouth Company two years ago he agreed with Stevens and Fell that they should serve the Company for 5 years and should be provided with a passage to New England, food, drink and clothing. Stevens was shipped as gunner and Fell as carpenter of the Little James and Governor Bradford had written a letter to confirm that their wages had been paid.

VOLUME 45 - UNFIT FOR PRODUCTION

VOLUME 46

RE THE JONATHAN. 31 May 1627.

Robert Gear of Weymouth, mariner aged 28. He was

Master of the Jonathan of Weymouth, 70 tons, which left there for New England in December 1625 for a fishing voyage after which she discharged her fish at Bordeaux. While she was there her sails and other equipment were removed to Bloy Castle.

----- **CROOKS v. CHRISTOPHER FORTUNE.** 11 & 21 August 1627.

Michael Marshall, citizen of London, merchant aged 39. He is owner of the Return and hired Giles Smith deceased to serve as steward on a voyage from Portsmouth to Virginia and return. Smith shipped tobacco from Virginia but, when the ship arrived in the Downs on her return, he went ashore and died. His tobacco went to the defendant. The deponent was in the ship for the whole voyage.

Hugh Weston of Wapping, Middlesex, sailor aged 28. Christopher Fortune was mate of the Return.

WILLIAM PULLMAN & JOHN DENNIS v. THE MARMADUKE. 26-31 October 1627.

Edward Singleton of Limehouse, Middlesex, scrivener aged 34. (2 examinations). He had kept the accounts of the Marmaduke since August 1625 when she was first built and was at Gravesend in August 1626 when she was provisioned and set sail for Virginia. John Dennis and other owners consented to the voyage and Edmond Pritchard, the purser, and Edmond Morgan, another owner, made a strict account of debts incurred in the provisioning of the ship by William Pullman. John Dennis, who was then aged, made the arrangements for the ship to be fitted out for the voyage.

Henry Baldwin, kinsman of William Pullman, aged 40.

VOLUME 47 - UNFIT FOR PRODUCTION

ENGLISH ADVENTURERS

VOLUME 48

RE THE ANNE OF PLYMOUTH. 24 March 1628/9.

Nicholas Harris of Plymouth, merchant aged 44. In February 1627/8 he received from Stephen Bray of the Anne of Plymouth an account of tobaccos loaded in her in Virginia on the deponent's account. The deponent, part owner of ship, brought off her tobacco and passengers when she arrived at St. Ives, Cornwall.

RE THE ANNE OF LONDON. 25 April & 6 May 1629.

Benjamin Moulson of Wapping, Middlesex, mariner aged 25. The Anne of London, Captain Peter Andrewes, loaded tobacco in Virginia in October 1628 for the account of Samuel Vassall of London, merchant. The deponent was boatswain of the ship and kept her books.

Rowland Powell, purser of the Anne, wrote out the bill of lading for the tobacco and was in the ship when she was taken.

WILLIAM EWENS v. THE SAKER. 6 May 1629.

William Dunn of Limehouse, Middlesex, sailor aged 39. The Saker arrived in Virginia in 1627 and delivered to William Ewen's plantation there only one passenger, a negro. The deponent was there with Captain Fellgate and they had authority to order the plantation.

Robert Penn of Virginia, planter aged 25, for Mr. Ewens whom he has known for 9 years. He was a planter on Ewens' plantation.

SAMUEL LANGHAM & THOMAS PHILLIPS v. FRANCIS GAWDEN. 10 May 1629 & 19 April 1630 (Vol. 49).

Robert Harris of St. Augustine, London, grocer aged 24,

servant of Samuel Langham whom he has known for 10 years. (2 examinations). The <u>Abigall</u> of Weymouth, of which Gawden was Master, loaded tobacco at Virginia for the account of the plaintiffs and brought it back to Weymouth where she arrived in February or March 1628/9. Jenkin Williams was sent to Weymouth to bring Langham's tobacco from the ship.

Edmund Peesly of St. Sepulchre, London, grocer aged 27, deposes as to tobacco prices in London.

Thomas Foote of St. Benet Gracechurch, London, grocer aged 32, also deposes as to tobacco prices.

Henry Tibbetts, apprentice of Samuel Langham, aged 18. Langham arranged for his tobacco to be collected from Weymouth.

RE THE PETER BONADVENTURE. 17 July & 28 September 1629, 14 & 15 April 1630 (Vol. 49).

Robert Kesteeven of Bermuda, schoolmaster aged 46, deposes for Michael Rickarde. When the <u>Peter Bonadventure</u> was in Bermuda in February 1628/9 she loaded tobacco for the account of Michael Rickarde, merchant of London, some of which was brought to the deponent by two Ministers in Bermuda, Patrick Copeland and George Stircke.

Robert Bailye of Limehouse, Middlesex, mariner aged 41. He was in charge of the boats which carried tobacco from shore to the <u>Peter Bonadventure</u> of London, Captain Thomas Sherwin. The deponent received tobacco from the wife of Abraham Sheeres, now dwelling in Whitechapel, and from Sheeres' father-in-law, both then dwelling in Bermuda. On her return voyage the ship was taken off Dartmouth by the Dunkerkers in April or May 1629.

John Earrington of Wapping, Middlesex, mariner aged 21. He was in Bermuda in March 1628/9 and loaded tobacco for the account of Mathewe Bateson whose factor in Bermuda was John Trimingham.

John Trimingham of the Somer Islands, merchant aged 40. The deponent Earrington was purser of the ship and this deponent has known the claimant Bateson for 30 years. The ship was taken and carried to Dunkirk.

RE JOHN RILEY. 26 August 1629.

Isabell, wife of William Perry, merchant of Virginia, aged 40. Last Christmas John Rily of London, merchant, lodged in her husband's house in Virginia and often said he was a partner in trade with William Crowther and Charles Whichcote of London, merchants. When he was in his last sickness, Rily arranged for her husband to mark tobaccos to be sent to John Holland and Rily's mother.

RE THE CARLILE. 21 January 1629/30.

Robert Dennys of Limehouse, Middlesex, mariner. He was Master of the Carlile and freighted goods and passengers belonging to the Earl of Carlisle to St. Christopher's, Barbados and Nevis before his ship was taken.

RE THE SUN.
11 March 1629/30 & 12 May 1630 (Vol.49).

Daniel Bidle/Beddell of All Hallows, Barking, London, mariner aged 34. When he was in Canada in May 1628 he was hired by Joseph Page, merchant of the Sun to go in her from Canada to Virginia. The ship belonged to Page and his father and was of 70 or 80 tons. She was so leaky that she had to be taken on shore in Canada to be made fit for the voyage to Virginia but the cause of her leakiness could not then be found. Joseph Page and William Lea then said that they had made many voyages in the Sun over a period of 5 years and during that time she had always been leaky. During their passage to Virginia the pumps had to be manned constantly. After her arrival in Virginia, her Master John Starr, the Mate John Frude, her carpenter, and William Lea died. Joseph Page asked the deponent to sell the ship but he could find no one in Virginia to buy her. Captain Mathewes, then resident in Virginia, said he would not give anything for her as she then lay sunk in harbour. The deponent, Joseph Page and one Sweet had travelled home in the London Merchant from Virginia, being afraid to come in the Sun. Captain Francis West, then Governor of Virginia, had ordered Page to release 14 passengers from their obligation to take passage in the Sun to England.

William Tucker Esq of Elizabeth City. The Sun of Plymouth arrived in Virginia with fish in August or September 1628, about 4 months before he left for England. When the planters who had intended to take passage in her for England learned of her condition they asked the Governor to be released from their obligation. On 8 December 1628 the deponent left Virginia in the Grace of Southampton and arrived at Plymouth on 2 February 1628/9. While he was still in Plymouth the Prudence of Stonehouse also docked and her Master, James Baker, reported that he had lost company with the Sun during a storm and feared she was lost.

VOLUME 49

RE THE JANE BONADVENTURE. 16 April 1630.

James Futter of London, merchant tailor aged 27. He was on the Jane Bonadventure of London, Mr. Thomas Randall, at Barbados on 28 July 1629 when tobacco was loaded for Augustine Futter & Francis Futter & Co. of London. While was at St. Christopher's the ship was taken by the Spanish fleet.

RE THE GIFT OF GOD. 25 May 1630 to 26 July 1631.

ENGLISH ADVENTURERS

William Barker of Ratcliffe, Middlesex, mariner aged 37. He was Mate of the Hopewell which sailed from Virginia on New Year's Eve 1629 for England under her Master Richard Russell and in company with the Gift of London, Captain Samuel Crampton and Master Edward Beale. The ships stayed together for 2 days and nights but were separated by a violent storm off Cape Hatteras since when the Gift had not been heard of.

Richard Atkins, planter of Virginia aged 29. He also came from Virginia on the Hopewell and deposes as above.

Thomas Burbidge/Burbage of St. Antholin, London, merchant tailor aged 24, deposes for Mr. Slayne. The Gift loaded tobacco at Kiekuotan in December 1629 on the account of the deponent and Captain William Peirce of Virginia. When she left Virginia the ship carried 50 men and boys.

Richard Russell of Ratcliffe, Middlesex, mariner aged 39. He loaded tobacco on the Gift of God in Virginia but came home in the Hopewell of London.

Francis Munden of Limehouse, Middlesex, mariner aged 22. He was not in Virginia when the Gift of God arrived there but knows she carried passengers and tobacco when she left there. He returned home in the Hopewell.

JOHN JONES v. ALEXANDER BANISTER. 12 & 28 June 1630.

John Cheshire of St. Dunstan in the West, London, gent aged 22. He went to Barbados with other passengers on the William, Mr. John Jones, of which the owners were Alexander Banister and William Perkins. When Jones went ashore at Barbados he was arrested and imprisoned for 2 days by order of the Governor, Captain (Henry) Powell. After his release he took his ship on to St. Christopher's where the deponent found his master Captain Wheatly with whom he returned on the William to Barbados where Wheatly had been appointed Governor in succession to Powell.

Nicholas Cage of Barbados, gent aged 36.

James Leeth of Ratcliffe, Middlesex, sailor aged 34. The William was chartered to carry Wheatly to Barbados where he was to remain and to take a different ship back to London. James Allen was hired to serve in the ship in which the deponent went as boatswain.

SAMUEL VASSALL v. WILLIAM GREENE.
9 July to 26 August 1630.

Peter Andrewes of Ratcliffe, Middlesex, sailor aged 33. He took goods and passengers to Virginia as Master of the Susan of Alborowe which Samuel Vassall chartered from the owners William Greene and John Wolverston. During her outward passage in October and November 1629 the ship was found to be in a rotten condition and very leaky and the pumps had to be continually manned for a period of 6 weeks. The passengers were exceedingly wet during most of the passage, the provisions were ruined, and the beds and rugs so rotted by damp that they had to be thrown overboard. When they arrived in Virginia the ship was hauled ashore to be refitted and, because there was not sufficient rope to be had there, some was taken out of the ship which had been consigned to Mr. Richard Stephens, a merchant in Virginia. One of the Susan's company, Mr. John Arnold, asserted that the ship was caulked in Virginia for the first time since her launch. Because she needed such extensive repairs the Susan was forced to stay in Virginia for 6 weeks before returning to England.

John Harcastell of Limehouse, Middlesex, sailor aged 27. The bulkheads of the Susan fell down and the middle deck in the great cabin sank by 2 inches.

ENGLISH ADVENTURERS

Robert Poddy of Ratcliffe, Middlesex, sailor aged 38. He was born in Tidnam, Gloucestershire, and has lived at Ratcliffe, Limehouse and at sea for 10 years. While the Susan was in Virginia another ship, the Friendship of London, was also carried ashore to staunch her leaks. With the exception of one person who fell overboard at night, all the Susan's passengers had been safely delivered to Virginia. Because of the state of the ship, of which the deponent was the carpenter, her Captain was obliged to hire two more carpenters in Virginia to return in her to London. Most of the company and passengers would willingly have lost all they had to be put ashore anywhere rather than to continue in daily fear and danger.

Peter Thomas of Limehouse, Middlesex, sailor aged 29. He was born in Guernsey and has lived there, in Southampton, at Limehouse and at sea for 10 years. He was a quartermaster of the Susan.

RE THE VINTAGE OF LONDON. 20 August 1630.

Thomas Burbage of St. Antholin, London, merchant aged 22. In May 1630 he shipped tobacco from Virginia on the Vintage for himself, Mr. John Walters and Captain Royden of London, merchant, and returned from Virginia in the ship himself.

RE THE PILGRIM OF LONDON. 23 & 24 August 1630.

William Worlich of Redriffe, Surrey, mariner aged 26. He went Master of the Pilgrim in August 1629 on a voyage to New England but the ship was seized off Canada by Captain Daniell of Dieppe who stripped her of her lading. On 31 October 1629 as she was returning to England she ran into foul weather off the Scilly Isles and her masts and sails were cut down to save her.

Nicholas Shevell of Shadwell, Middlesex, mariner aged 26. He was quartermaster of the ship which was forced to put into Ireland on her return voyage.

John Smyth of Ratcliffe, Middlesex, sailor aged 21. He served on the <u>Pilgrim</u>.

RE JOHN RAYMOND. 15 September 1630.

Patrick Kennedy of Redriffe, Surrey, mariner aged 40. John Raymond was Master's Mate of the <u>Friendship</u> of London and died while she was on passage to Virginia having made the deponent and Humphrey Barrett overseers of his will. The deponent sold Raymond's goods in Virginia and shipped back tobacco which he delivered to his widow.

Humphrey Barrett of Wapping, Middlesex, mariner aged 50, deposes similarly.

RE THE SWIFT OF BRISTOL. 5 October to 1 November 1630.

Stephen Reeke of Poole, Dorset, mariner aged 24. In April 1630 he was hired by Mr. Thomas Wright, merchant of Bristol, to serve in the <u>Swift</u>, 70 tons, for a voyage from Bristol to New England. The ship was freighted and provisioned by Mr. Vines, servant of Sir Ferdinando Gorges, and by Mr. Alderton, a dweller in New England, and Thomas Wright. Her passengers and goods were delivered in New England in July 1630. On 10 August while the ship was at Monteggan (?<u>Monhegan Island</u>) in New England she loaded fish and oil to be delivered to Wright's factor on St. Michael's Island and then to return to Bristol. But on 19 August 1630 she was seized by the bark <u>Warwick</u> under Captain Weatherley.

James Nicholls of Milbrooke, Cornwall, navigator aged 26. He and 4 others were put aboard the <u>Swift</u> at Moggegan (<u>sic</u>) to bring her to England but when they reached Bristol her company confessed that she had been intended for St. Michael's Island in the King of

ENGLISH ADVENTURERS

Spain's dominions.

Thomas Millard of Shadwell, Middlesex, sailor aged 35. He was Master of a shallop engaged in trade along the New England coast and went aboard the Swift while she was in Damrell's Cove (?Damariscotta) in New England before she was taken. There he saw the ship's journal which clearly showed she was bound for St. Michael's, having left some passengers from Bristol at Sawco. The deponent was told that the Swift had already been sold to the Portuguese before she left Bristol and that, after her voyage to New England, both her name and that of her Master would be changed.

Thomas Hardy of Barrow in Furness, Scotland, sailor aged 24. He had heard the Swift's Master when he was drunk tell Weatherley that his ship was bound to St. Michael's.

RE THE JANE OF LONDON. 1 & 3 March 1630/31.

Robert Hynd of St. Bride, London, gent aged 45, deposes for Augustus Flutter. In May 1630 tobacco was loaded on the Jane, Captain Henry Stratford, by Richard Minns or Minnis and John Bray and taken to Ireland where part was sold.

Samuel Lee of Ratcliffe, Middlesex, mariner aged 30, was Master of the Jane and deposes similarly.

RICHARD TAYLOR v. ZACHARY CRAVEN. 24 March & 11 May 1631.

Nicholas Herne of St. Giles, Cripplegate, London, draper aged 37. Richard Taylor, Master of the Hunter of Dover, and Zachary Craven, factor for Robert Craven, loaded tobacco on the ship at St. Christopher's and Barbados which was to be delivered to Robert Craven in London.

William Banckes, citizen and goldsmith of London aged

33. He was at the Custom House in London when the tobacco was received from the Hunter.

EDWARD BOOMER v. HENRY GARDINER. 21 & 24 May 1631.

Richard Wilson of Wapping, Middlesex, sailor aged 29. In February 1627/8 Edward Boomer hired Hugh Greve as his apprentice to serve on the Faith of London, Mr. Robert Watson, for a voyage to Virginia and back to England. Henry Gardiner paid the wages of the ship's company.

Thomas Taunton of Wapping, Middlesex, sailor aged 38. He was carpenter of the Faith on which Greve served until her return to Dartmouth.

RE THE DONCASTER OF LONDON. 19 December 1631.

Jonas Colbach, late Secretary to the Governor and Council of St. Christopher's in the West Indies, aged 43. On 15 December 1630 when he was at St. Christopher's he delivered tobacco to Jeffery Cartwright, purser of the Doncaster, to be delivered to Francis Johnson of London.

Thomas Offley of St. James, Dukes Place, London, merchant tailor aged 32. He was purser of the Doncaster in October 1630 when her Master, Francis Johnson, loaded her with tobacco at Barbados and Nevis.

DAVID KIRK & CANADA CO. v. EUSTACE MAN. 23 January 1631/2 to 19 July 1632.

Vincent Harris of St. Peter le Poer, London, gent aged 29. Captain David Kirk and others, adventurers to Canada, have been prejudiced in their trade by Captain Man, Captain West & Co., adventurers in the Elizabeth of London in her voyage to Canada. When the deponent was there on Kirk's behalf the Indians in that place refused to trade because they had already done business with the Elizabeth of which James Ricrafte was the merchant and pilot.

William Holmes of St. Peter ad Vincula within the Tower of London, gent aged 32, deposes similarly. He was purser of the Thomas of London, Captain Vincent Harris, which was in the Gulf of Canada while the Elizabeth Bonadventure was also there.

Maurice Thomson of St. Andrew, Eastcheap, London, aged 27. The Whale of London, Mr. Richard Brereton, owned by Mathew Cradocke and Nathaniel Wright of London, merchants, and by a Mr. Phillips of London, voyaged to the coast of Canada during the past 12 months and after a visit to St. Christopher's returned to the Thames in December 1631.

Miles Knowles of St. Olave, Southwark, Surrey, haberdasher aged 43. In May 1631 he and Thomas Barrett, haberdasher, bought beaver and skins from Eustace Man which Barrett and his father-in-law Mr. Man sold to John Wayborne, Samuel Peirce, Richard and Thomas Barnes, William Daniel and Edward Austen, beavermakers near Bridewell.

Edward Wiggins, Messenger of His Majesty's Chamber. In October 1631 James Ricrafte was committed to prison by order of the Privy Council. When John Delabarr said that he intended to send Ricrafte to sea he was informed that he could not. Maurice Thomson well knew that Ricrafte was a prisoner.

Thomas Smyth of Redriffe, Surrey, mariner aged 40. In February 1627/8 Captain Kirk and other adventurers to Canada sent a fleet of 3 ships there: the Abigall, Captain David Kirk; the Charity, Captain Thomas Kirk; and the Elizabeth, Captain Hutchins. They returned to England in September 1628.

In 1629 a fleet of 8 ships was sent: the Abigall, Captain David Kirk; the George, Captain Thomas Kirk; the William, Captain Michell, a Frenchman; the Jarvas,

Captain Richard Brereton; the Robert, of which the deponent was Captain; the Thomas, Captain Swanton; the Charles, Captain Jenkins; and a small pinnace of which Thomas Witherlye was Master. In March 1630 2 further ships were sent: the Robert, Captain Thomas Kirk, and the Thomas, Captain Richard Brereton. In March 1631 2 ships were sent: the Robert of which the deponent went Captain, and the Thomas, Captain Vincent Harris.

Edward Churchwell of Ratcliffe, Middlesex, mariner aged 24. He went to Canada in the Elizabeth of London, Mr. John Baker. In May 1631 the Thomas of London, Captain Vincent Harris, arrived there and returned to London the following September.

Thomas Rearer of Limehouse, Middlesex, sailor aged 24. He went to Canada as Mate of the Thomas.

Peter Pett of Deptford, Kent, shipwright aged 39. In 1631 he was employed by Sir Robert Mansfield, Vice Admiral of England, to sell a Dutch pink called the Peter of 60 tons which was purchased by Captain Eustace Man of the Isle of Wight who fitted her with another deck and re-named her the Elizabeth. Man is reputed to be her sole owner. (Vol. 50).

Eustace Man of the Isle of Wight, Esq aged 54. (Vol. 50).

VOLUME 50

RE THE FALCON. 23 June to 10 July 1632.

Francis Smyth of Wapping, Middlesex, mariner aged 36. He was steward of the Falcon, Mr. William Douglas, which left Tilbury for Virginia on 12 August 1631 with old and worn rigging and equipment. While she was in Virginia a refit had to be carried out to make the ship safe for her return voyage, otherwise her company would not have returned in her. While she was anchored between Hogg Island and Mulberry Island in James River she broke loose from her moorings and was driven ashore. Her cargo had to be unloaded before she could be pulled off. On her return voyage the ship leaked badly and her tobacco was spoiled.

John Hogge of Wapping, Middlesex, mariner aged 24. He went as boatswain of the Falcon and made out a note of her deficiencies which he gave to one of the ship's owners, James Woodcott.

Raphe Atkinson of Southampton, mariner aged 47. He was Master's Mate of the Falcon.

Daniel Jones of Ratcliffe, Middlesex, ship carpenter aged 22. He went as carpenter's mate of the Falcon.

Thomas Todd of Wapping, Middlesex, ship carpenter aged 22. He was chief carpenter of the Falcon during her return voyage to London.

RE THE PHILIP OF LONDON, 2 September 1632.

John Babb of Ratcliffe, Middlesex, mariner aged 39. He was Master of the Phillip of London, 140 tons, which was chartered by William Felgate, Morrice Thomson and others of London, merchants, from the owners Giles Yates & Co. for a voyage to Virginia in June 1630. The ship arrived there in August 1630 where she loaded tobacco. On 1 January 1630/31 she sailed for home but in the middle of that month encountered a great storm in which she lost much of her equipment and rigging. In early February she was driven into the Scillies.

DAVID KIRK & CO. v. JOHN ALLEN & CO.
DAVID KIRK v. JOHN SEAMAN.
10 August 1632 to 13 February 1632/3.

Alexander Rive of St. Katherine by the Tower, London, cooper aged 34. David Kirk & Co. freighted the Phoenix for a voyage from Yarmouth to Newfoundland and Canada and home to London. The deponent went as cooper and believes the ship was not fit for sea.

ENGLISH ADVENTURERS

Because she became leaky she had to be hauled ashore in Canada in order to fit her for the return voyage.

Thomas Wadham of Stepney, Middlesex, sailor aged 26, deposes about the charter party between David Kirk and the owners of the ship including John Allen.

John Bilton of Redriffe, Surrey, sailor aged 23. He went as carpenter of the Phoenix.

Samuel Parratt of ?Bondreun, Devon, sailor aged 31. He had heard the owners say the Phoenix was chartered to her Master, John Currell, for a voyage to Newfoundland. While she was in Canada David Kirk and his brother Thomas Kirk were obliged to hire men to bring her ashore for repairs.

Robert Biles of Limehouse, Middlesex, sailor aged 48, deposes as above.

John Crosthwaite, sometime preacher to the English colony in Canada, aged 32. He went to Canada with Captain Lewis Kirk when he took the Fort of Quebec some 3 years ago, and left in July 1632 when the Fort was surrendered to the French. Nicholas Phelps took an inventory of the goods saved from the fire at Quebec a year ago, some of which fell into the hands of Captain Thomas Kirk who, with the deponent and others, landed at Deal, Kent, on their return from Canada. During the deponent's first 2 years in Canada, Captain Lewis Kirk was in command of all trade there and during the last year Captain Thomas Kirk controlled it.

Henry Burgis of St. Cleeve, Cornwall, mariner aged 32. He went to Canada in June 1631 as quartermaster of the Jonas of London, Mr. John Crowther. He deposes about the loading of the Phoenix at Quebec and trade in Canada.

Marles Twine of Stepney, Middlesex, mariner aged 22. He went from London to Canada in the Jonas 16 months ago and while he was in Quebec Captain

ENGLISH ADVENTURERS

Thomas Kirk was Governor there. He deposes about the goods put aboard ships in Quebec and trade in Canada.

Nicholas Phelps of All Hallows, Barking, London, merchant aged 28. (2 depositions). He went to Canada in the Jonas and remained there until she returned in July 1632. He was in Canada when the Phoenix arrived there and was appointed by Thomas Kirk to keep a magazine in Quebec. Another magazine was kept by a Frenchman, John Bally.

Richard Currell of Redriffe, Surrey, mariner aged 27. He has made 3 voyages to Canada on behalf of the Canada Company but has never resided there.

Malachy Greete of Wapping, Middlesex, mariner aged 25. He has made 4 voyages to Canada for the Company and has lived for 9 months ashore in Quebec.

Richard Hunter of St. Sepulchre, London, clerk aged 62. He has made 3 voyages to Canada for the Company. Trade there was controlled by Bally, Maslett, Philips, John Lowe and James Hensfield and "no man durst trade there openly but the Company's factors."

George Taply of St. Botolph, Aldgate, London, mariner aged 34, gunner of the Robert. He has made two voyages to Canada and after his first voyage lived ashore there for 2 years.

Joseph Dobbins of Redriffe, Surrey, mariner aged 22, coxswain of the Robert. He has made 3 voyages to Canada but has never resided there.

Thomas Witherly of Horsley Down, Surrey, mariner aged 30. He has made 2 voyages to Canada and on the second lived ashore for almost a year.

William Hammon of Wapping, Middlesex, mariner, a quartermaster of the Robert. He has made 2 voyages to Canada but has not resided there.

ENGLISH ADVENTURERS

James Hensfield of Dieppe, France, mariner aged 26, Master's Mate of the <u>Robert</u>. He has made only one voyage to Canada where he lived ashore in the Company's service for 2 years and traded with the savages at Todosacke. The goods brought out of Quebec after the fire were taken to London.

William White of Redriffe, Surrey, mariner, a quartermaster of the <u>Robert</u>, aged 38. He has made 4 voyages to Canada in the <u>Robert</u> but has never resided on shore there.

Samuel Hardinge of St. Thomas, Southwark, Surrey, cooper aged 37. He has made 4 voyages to Canada but has never lived ashore there.

William Favour of London, girdler aged 31. He has made 2 voyages to Canada and lived ashore for 3 months in Quebec.

Peter Rey of Paris, France, master carpenter aged 48. He has made only one voyage to Canada on behalf of the Company and lived there for 3 years. Iron ware and other items which were not consumed in the fire at Quebec were committed to the care of the Company's factor John Balley who afterwards delivered them to M. de Cane.

Pliney Warde of Redriffe, Surrey, mariner aged 45. He has made 4 voyages to Canada, 2 being to Quebec and 2 to Todosack, but has not resided ashore. The <u>Phoenix</u> went from Todosack to Quebec leaving the <u>Robert</u> at Todosack.

Christopher Stagge of Redriffe, Surrey, sailor aged 26. He was at Quebec when the Fort was taken by Kirk and has made 3 voyages to Canada but never resided ashore.

Ambrose Baker of Redriffe, Surrey, mariner aged 32. He has made 4 voyages to Canada but has not lived ashore there.

ENGLISH ADVENTURERS

George Clarke of Gosport, Hants, mariner aged 40. He has made 5 voyages to Canada, 4 of them to Quebec, but has not lived ashore there.

John Lowe of St. Giles, Cripplegate, London, merchant tailor aged 50. He has made 4 voyages to Canada and has spent some time ashore there.

Thomas Smith of Redriffe, Surrey, mariner aged 41. He has made 4 voyages to Canada but has not lived ashore there.

Henry Kinge of Redriffe, Surrey, mariner aged 45. He has made 3 voyages to Canada but has not lived ashore there.

Thomas Jacobs of Dieppe, France, brewer aged 19. He has lived in Canada for 2 years, having been sent there by Kirk & Co. to live with the savages, learn their language and act as an interpreter for trade. With 62 other Frenchmen in the service of French merchants trading in Quebec, he was shipped on the Lyon for Dieppe but, 4 or 5 weeks after they had set sail, they were cast away on the coast of Brittany. Most of the beaver skins on the ship were saved but were then pillaged by the French.

Isaac Helme of St. Mary Axe, London, barber aged 25. He lived for 4 years in Canada in the Company's service and sometimes went into the country with Thomas Jacobs and Peter Geantott to trade with the savages. He left Quebec in the Lyon for Dieppe.

John Correll the elder of Redriffe, Surrey, sailor aged 60. He went Master of the Phoenix to Canada for which voyage the charter party was drawn up between David Kirk, William Berkeley and Joshua Galliard and the owners John Seaman, Samuel Dubbleday, Paul Cooke and John Allen.

John Correll of Redriffe, Surrey, sailor aged 24. He went to Canada as Master's Mate of the Phoenix and has seen a letter from Captain David Kirk to his father commissioning him to find a ship at Ipswich or Yarmouth suitable for a voyage to Canada.

Peter Garnetot of St. Mure du Lossoi in Burgundy, France, tanner aged 32. He has lived for 6 years in Canada, 3 years in the service of the French and 3 in the service of English merchants, trading with the savages. There were 60 people in the service of the French under the orders of M. de Cane and Captain de Lakada and these were shipped on the Lyon for France and cast away near Basse Froide in Brittany on 24 October 1632.

RE THE ELIZABETH OF LONDON. 30 January to 7 February 1632/3. (see also **BRADSHAW v. THE SPEELE** p.87).

Francis Browne of Shadwell, Middlesex, mariner aged 36. He was Master of the Elizabeth under Captain Richard Bradshawe which loaded goods and passengers for New England and, on 1 April 1632, anchored under H.M. Fort at Pendennis, Cornwall. A fleet of Dutch ships arrived there and one of them, the Compass of Horne, heaved an anchor under the Elizabeth and holed her so that she could not continue her voyage. The Dutch ship was put under arrest but made her escape.

Roger Bradshawe of St. Bride, London, joiner aged 34.

James Johnson of St. Andrew, Holborn, London, exciseman aged 36. He was a passenger on the Elizabeth bound for New England. The ship had been fitted out by Captain Richard Bradshawe, Captain Eustace Mann and Captain Henry West.

EDWARD THOMPSON v. JOHN DELABARR. 17 June 1633.

William Copeland of Wapping, Middlesex, sailor aged 30. He went as Master's Mate in the Endeavour, Mr. James Ricrafte, chartered from Edward Thompson for Canada.

ENGLISH ADVENTURERS

While they were in Canada, Thompson traded for furs and skins contrary to the wishes of Delabarr and Ricrafte.

JOHN MASON v. JOHN GIBBS & GIBBS v. MASON. 15 November to 6 December 1632.

Stephen Simons of Plymouth, Devon, sailor aged 33. He served as carpenter on the Lion's Whelp of 90 tons, Mr. John Gibbs, for a fishing voyage to New England in January 1631/2. The ship was chartered by John Mason & Co. Because she was defective and leaky they experienced a difficult voyage of 12 weeks and did not arrive in New England until the fishing season was almost over. On the return voyage they had to put in at Plymouth because of contrary winds.

John True of Shadwell, Middlesex, sailor aged 27. He is worth £30 and now lodges at Shadwell in the house of Widow Reeves but was born at Langton, Dorset, and lived there until 5 years ago, but has since gone to sea in merchant affairs. On her outward voyage the Lion's Whelp embarked 4 passengers in London for New England: a man and his wife, their 2 daughters, and a young man. These were not intended for Captain John Mason's plantation. The ship arrived at the Isle of Shoals in New England in May 1632 and, on her return voyage, 6 passengers were embarked besides such as came from Mason's plantation.

Benjamin Bowden of Ratcliffe, Middlesex, sailor aged 30. A man and his wife, their 2 daughters and their man were embarked for New England on behalf of Matthew Craddock.

Henry Coolinge of St. Martin le Vintry, London, merchant aged 46. He is worth £20 and was formerly, but not now, a subsidy man, and dwells as St. Martin Orgars in Thames Street, London, and uses the trade of merchandizing. He went to New England as purser of the Lion's Whelp of which the owners were Matthew Craddock, Robert Holland and John Gibbs, and she was chartered by John Mason & Co. and John Cotton. Eight passengers, including one named Captain Pettifaye, were shipped from London to New England, and 10 were shipped for the return voyage of whom 4 were of Captain Mason's company. Several plants were shipped in tubs on the outward passage to be planted at Mason's plantation but, being ruined by sea water, they were thrown overboard.

William Hickson of St. George, Southwark, Surrey, citizen and tallow chandler of London aged 26. He went as cook on the Lion's Whelp and heard the purser, Henry Coolinge, complain of waste on the ship. The deponent has made only 2 voyages to sea and was never before on a fishing voyage.

Robert Bray of St. Olave, Southwark, Surrey, shipwright aged 20. Captain Neale employed the ship's carpenter, Stephen Symons, to repair a pinnace on shore in New England.

Robert Doves of St. Olave, Southwark, Surrey, shipwright aged 17. He was not hired to serve in the ship but went as a common man. Before leaving New England, Captain Mason spared some of his ship's beer to another vessel there called the Pied Cow and sent other beer to his plantation in New England.

RICHARD BRERETON v. CHARLES ATYE. 1 July to 13 August 1633.

Thomas Eyre of St. Dionysius Backchurch, London, merchant aged 57. In September 1630 he was Treasurer of the Canada Company, of which Charles Atye is a member, and calculated wages due to Richard Brereton as Master of the Thomas for a voyage to Canada.

William Cloberry of St. Andrew Hubbard, London, merchant aged 38. Richard Brereton made one voyage to Canada on behalf of the Canada Company as Master of the Thomas.

ENGLISH ADVENTURERS

Thomas Wannerton of St. Mary Woolnoth, London, notary public. On 22 May 1633 Thomas Eyre, Treasurer of the Canada Company, sold to Robert Clements of London, shipwright, a ship formerly called the <u>Joseph</u> of Dieppe but now the <u>Thomas</u> of London.

ROBERT SOUTH & MAURICE THOMPSON v. ----- KINGE. Examinations made in 1633 re the disposition of tobaccos brought to London in the <u>Charity</u>, Mr. Richard Lowe. One examinant declared that South had refused to take delivery of his tobacco saying: "It was a base drug and he had disbursed and laid out more money upon tobacco than he thought he should ever see again."

Thomas Murthwaite, examined on behalf of South, deposed that it was usual when ships came from St. Christopher's and Virginia, before they came into English waters, to send their tobacco for Holland to seek a market for it if prices in England were low.

----- BROOKE & CO. v. ROBERT OFFLEY, ----- MASON & RICHARD PHILPOTT. 24 October 1633 etc.

Francis Grigge of Gosport near Portsmouth, Hants, shipwright aged 22. The <u>Anne and Frances</u>, Mr. Robert Offley, was hauled on shore at Gosport where she was resheathed and a new deck fitted for a voyage to St. Christopher's. She then put into Plymouth to join the <u>Charity</u> for the voyage, and later, because of bad weather, into the Scillies. When she reached St. Christopher's and had landed her goods and passengers, Offley declared his intention of trading in other islands to pick up tobacco. One of the ship's freighters, Richard Philpott, declared he would rather trade for hides but, after a month at St. Christopher's, the ship loaded salt at St. Martin's. While giving chase to a Spanish ship, the <u>Anne and Frances</u> ran aground at St. Cruce and became leaky thereafter. Because Offley refused to make a merchant voyage to Virginia, the chief mate, Stephen Worsley, the ship's surgeon, carpenter and quartermaster left her at Tartoogas. Others wanted to leave the ship at Barbados because of the shortage of victuals. The Anne and Frances arrived back in Falmouth and Portsmouth very leaky and worm eaten.

RE THE WILLIAM OF LONDON. 5-7 November 1633.

Andrew Hume of St. Katherine by the Tower, London, mariner aged 32. In December 1632 William Clobery, David Morehead and John Delabarr freighted the William, Mr. William Trevore, to trade for skins in Hudson's Bay adjoining Virginia where she arrived on 13 April 1633. There the Dutch boarded her and commanded her crew to go ashore to their fort. They were afterwards allowed to proceed up river where Jacob Jacobson Elkins and other merchants went on shore, pitched their tent, and began to trade with the natives. But the Dutch, who had followed them, intervened, pulled down the tent, and forced the William to return down river.

William Forde of Limehouse, Middlesex, mariner aged 36. He went as gunner of the ship.

Richard Barnard of Wapping, Middlesex, sailor aged 26. He went as quartermaster.

John Johnson of St. Botolph, Aldgate, London, citizen and cordwainer of London aged 45. He went as cook of the William which was victualled for a voyage to Plymouth in New England where she was to land her passengers and then go on to Hudson's Bay.

Jacob Jacobson Elkins of Amsterdam, merchant aged 42. He went as ship's factor. The Dutchmen who wrought injury upon the William were Walter Vertrill, Governor of Amsterdam Fort, John van Remont, the Governor's Secretary, Martyn Garretson, Conrade Noteman Ahuddus, Captain Jacob Johnson Hesse, all counsellors to the Governor, and Hance Jorison Honten, Governor of Fort Orange.

WILLIAM CANTRELL v. MATTHEW SMALLWOOD.   9 November 1633 to 24 October 1634.

Patrick Kennede of Redriffe, Surrey, sailor aged 45. He was pilot of the Unicorn which loaded tobacco at Blunt Point in the River of Virginia from November to January 1630/31.   Matthew Smallwood, factor for Captain John Prynn who was one of the ship's freighters, signed most of the bills of lading and acted as ship's purser. Henry Cantrell came from Virginia as a passenger in the ship.

Oliver Henly of St. Mary Woolchurch, London, haberdasher aged 61.   He and William Cantrell are countrymen and therefore loving friends.   Henry Cantrell consigned tobacco by the Unicorn to William Cantrell who never received it.   In September 1631 the deponent sent some tobacco from the same ship to Haviland Hiley, a shopkeeper in Poole, Dorset.

Peter Prestwood of St. Michael, Cornhill, London, clothworker aged 34.   In 1632 Thomas Higgins who lived at Tunstall, Staffordshire, lodged in his house and purchased tobacco from William Cantrell which was alleged to have been sent to him by his brother Henry Cantrell, a planter in Virginia.

John Bradstreet of the Tower Precinct, London, tallow chandler aged 32.   A person named Hardcastle loaded Virginia tobacco on the Christopher and Mary, Mr. Peter Andrewes, consigned to John Punchard of Limehouse, Middlesex, mariner, which was delivered to his wife Mrs. Punchard.   The deponent is examined as to tobacco prices in London. (Vol. 51).

Barnabas Cutts of St. Andrew, Holborn, London, scissor merchant aged 42.   He was employed as a tobacco broker and in 1631 sold Virginia tobacco on behalf of Reginald Parker, linen draper in Tower Street, to Gabriel Bonner, grocer against St. Sepulchre's Church; and on behalf of Mr. Michael Herringe, merchant dwelling in Walbrook, to Mr. William Tickner, grocer in Red Cross Street.   In 1632 he sold Virginia tobacco on behalf of Captain John Preene to Tickner. (Vol. 51).

GEORGE THOMPSON v. CHRISTOPHER DIGHTON & RICHARD STARCHYE. 9 December 1633 to 8 February 1633/4.

Thomas Ramsey of St. Olave, Southwark, Surrey, sailor aged 44. He was hired by Jeremy Blackman, Master of the Expedition bound from London to Virginia, to pilot her to the Downs. When the ship arrived at Gravesend, Kent, on 19 July 1633, Christopher Dighton, the Searcher there, came aboard and required all the passengers to take the Oath of Allegiance and demanded head money for all of them. George Thompson, merchant, one of the freighters, told Dighton that he had never paid head money for passengers to Virginia and offered him a bond instead. Dighton was not satisfied with this and had the ship arrested, putting a broad arrow on her mainmast. A boat was sent to the ship to ferry passengers ashore to take the Oath of Allegiance and on the following day a man was sent aboard to administer the Oath to other passengers. The ship was detained until 20 July and thereby lost her wind for the Downs, by which Thompson & Co. were greatly damnified, there being a great number of passengers aboard the ship. The deponent had never known any other ship pay head money to the Searcher of Gravesend for passengers to Virginia, though it was usual for strangers bound to Holland or France.

Richard Grove of St. Olave, Southwark, Surrey, navigator aged 38. He was hired by Thompson to carry a great number of people in his barge from London to Gravesend to embark in the Expedition as passengers. George Thompson and his brother Maurice Thompson had traded to Virginia for many years but head money had never before been demanded of them. A great horse boat was sent by the Searchers at Gravesend to fetch passengers to take the Oath of Allegiance and the deponent heard George Thompson say to Dighton that if any went missing he would hold Dighton responsible.

ENGLISH ADVENTURERS

William Tucker of Redriffe, Surrey, Esq. aged 44. He was part owner of the Expedition and was aboard her at Gravesend when the Searchers there, Christopher Dighton and Richard Starchye, claimed 6 pence a head as head money for each passenger and 3 pence a head to administer the Oath of Allegiance. The deponent has traded to Virginia for 23 years, has lived there, and is one of the Council there, and in all that time has never heard of head money being demanded except in the last 2 years since Dighton became the Gravesend Searcher. Because of the delays incurred the ship did not leave Plymouth until 26 August 1633. The Expedition is a ship of 300 tons and carried 100 passengers and 30 seamen.

John Bradstreet of St. Peter ad Vincula, London, citizen and tallow chandler of London, aged 32. He made out indentures and covenants for some of the passengers and took papers from London to Gravesend to clear the ship. He had received a letter from one of the passengers on the Expedition dated Plymouth, 24 August 1633.

SIR RICHARD SALTINSTALL v. JOHN TAYLER. 11 February 1633/4 to 14 May 1635.

Nicholas Trevise of Wapping, Middlesex, sailor aged 36. He was appointed by William Pearse to be Master of a ship formerly called the Thomas but now the Richard of London for a voyage to New England. She was delivered to John Tayler, shipwright, to be fitted out for the voyage at Nehemiah Bourne's dock. Sir Richard Saltinstall and his company set out on their voyage in June or July 1633 but the ship proved to be leaky and was forced to return to England where she was sold and her passengers reimbursed.

Samuel Harsenett of St. Bartholomew by the Exchange, London, grocer aged 42. He was appointed by Sir Richard Saltinstall to purchase a ship for the voyage to New England.

William Pearce/Peirce of Boston, New England, sailor aged 43. He has known Saltinstall for 6 years and John Tayler for 15. He was asked by John Humfreys, Saltinstall's partner, to find a ship suitable for a voyage to New England but, distrusting his own skill and judgement in such matters, sought Tayler's assistance. The latter recommended a ship in the Thames named the Thomas but, when the deponent saw her, he thought her old and rotten. A further visit to the ship was made in company with Tayler's brother and William Willoughby and on that occasion Tayler told the deponent that he might have a good pennyworth if he would buy her. The deponent then agreed to the purchase but only on condition that the Thomas was made fit for the proposed voyage and was taken to Nehemiah Bourne's dock for the purpose. Saltinstall had suffered loss through the ship's leakiness and the subsequent cancellation of her voyage for which she had embarked 20 passengers at £5 a head. Saltinstall and his partners John Humfreys, Mr. Atherton Hough, Nicholas Parker and Edward Buckley had appointed Nicholas Trevise as Master of the ship and Benjamin Gillam as her carpenter. (Vol. 51).

----- **BEANE v. SIR DAVID KIRK.** 1 October 1634 to 4 June 1635.

James Ricroft of Ratcliffe, Middlesex, mariner aged 33. He was appointed by Sir David Kirk and his adventurers to go as Master of the Mary Fortune on a trading voyage from London to the Canada River alias the Great River of St. Lawrence. He sailed from London on 4 March 1633/4 and arrived at Bonaventure in the Gulf of Canada on 22 April from where he proceeded to St. John's. On 8 May the ship arrived at Todosacke in the Canada River and was engaged by two French ships. After a fight the French took off all the Mary Fortune's goods and seamen to the fort at Quebec and took the ship herself to Dieppe.

Ruben Broad of Redriffe, Surrey, mariner aged 64. He was chief mate of the Mary Fortune which was freighted by Sir David Kirk, William Barkley and Joseph Galliard & Co.

Lewes Tucker of Wapping, Middlesex, mariner aged 26. (2 depositions). He was gunner's mate of the Mary Fortune.

George Smyth of Limehouse, Middlesex, mariner aged 24. (2 depositions). He was the boatswain of the Mary Fortune and after being released in Dieppe arrived home in September 1634.

William Davies of Wapping, Middlesex, ship carpenter aged 26. (2 depositions). He went as ship's carpenter.

William Rand of Stepney, Middlesex, mariner aged 39. (2 depositions). He was part owner and Master of the Mary Fortune before Ricroft and comes to depose at the request of Richard Cray and Edward Crosse.

Samuel Hardinge of St. Katherine by the Tower, London, cooper aged 35. He went as ship's cooper.

EDWARD KINGSWELL v. SAMUEL VASSALL. 7 November 1634 to 24 April 1635.

In **JOHN DEARSLYE v. SAMUEL VASSALL** examinations were made in November 1632 (Vol. 50) to establish what repairs had been carried out on the Mayflower of which Vassall was the owner and Peter Andrewes the Master.

Edward Purrier of Ratcliffe, Middlesex, mariner aged 45. He went as boatswain of the Mayflower, Mr. Peter Andrewes, on a voyage from London to Virginia and back in 1633 and 1634. The ship was as well victualled as any on which he had served in the last 20 years. For every mess of 5 persons there was allowed a quarter can of beer at every meal, and sometimes between meals when the weather was hot, 5 biscuits or, when they were gone, the equivalent in broken bread.

ENGLISH ADVENTURERS

On Tuesdays, Thursdays and Sundays beef and pease were provided and on Mondays, Wednesdays, Fridays and Saturdays, fish and oil or fish and butter. Almost every day on the voyage he saw the ship's company and passengers at dinner and supper and during his previous 3 voyages to Virginia never saw better or more plentiful victuals. So great was the allowance to passengers that they sometimes did not eat all that they had and several times when he called them to prayer (as it was his place to do) he observed fish lying in platters in the passengers' cabins which was sweet and wholesome. Though some passengers threw their fish overboard they would not have done so had sufficient victuals been wanting. When the ship was loaded at Plymouth the London beer was found to be lying so low in the ship with so many things heaped upon it that access to it was made inconvenient and Peter Andrewes arranged for a hogshead of Mr. (Edward) Kingswell's beer to be taken aboard which was replaced when the ship reached Virginia. Only one person had been taken sick during the voyage and that was one of Samuel Vassall's own servants.

One passenger who was accused of theft during the voyage was brought before Andrewes for punishment but, when one of Kingswell's men swore that if he were touched the passengers would throw all the seamen overboard, Andrewes desisted lest there should be a mutiny. The <u>Mayflower</u> weighs 400 tons when laden and draws 16 feet of water.

It was usual for all ships sailing to Virginia and the West Indies to provide beverages in hot weather and on the <u>Mayflower</u> a mixture of cider and water was distributed. The passengers did not labour aboard but went to sleep when they pleased. The deponent never heard of anyone on the voyage who drank salt water or his own urine because of lack of drink. Only one man had died on passage and that was from a calenture, and Mr. Andrewes had many times asked the ship's surgeon, Clement East, to take special care of the sick. More men usually died on the passage to Virginia than the one who died on the <u>Mayflower</u>, and her passengers

ENGLISH ADVENTURERS

were well and lusty when they were landed.

John Brasier of St. Giles, Cripplegate, London, shipwright aged 25. He went as carpenter of the Mayflower and had voyaged for 8 years as a carpenter but during that time had made only one previous voyage to Virginia, also in the Mayflower. He had seen one Hastings, servant to Mr. Kingswell, take 7 quarter cans of beer to his master in the great cabin. Mr. Kingswell's maidservant, Dorothy, who was sick during the voyage was given extra beer by the surgeon. One passenger named Owen had two dishes of beer allowed him at every meal, one of which he used to exchange with other passengers for biscuit: he then went on deck, made water in his hat or cap and drank his own urine, but not for want of drink.

When John Ripley saw one of the passengers taken before Andrewes to be punished for theft he exclaimed: "Zounds, shall we see our men punished thus? If you will be ruled by me we will throw all the seamen overboard."

The deponent had heard that when Captain Douglas's ship came to Virginia a little before the Mayflower, 8 passengers in her had died out of 150 on board whereas only one had died on the Mayflower which carried 300 passengers and seamen.

Thomas Hance of Wapping, Middlesex, sailor aged 27. He went as a common seaman in the Mayflower. While she was at Virginia several other English ships were also there: the Primrose of London, Captain Douglas; the Expedition of London, Mr. Jeremy Blackman; the Blessing of London, Mr. Seaverne, and 2 other ships of London of which the Masters were Smyth and Walker. None of them had provided greater allowances of food and drink than the Mayflower. The deponent had never heard Peter Andrewes say he would kick any woman in his ship nor give one ill language.

William Griffin of Ratcliffe, Middlesex, sailor aged 24. He served as a common man on the Mayflower and was never before in a ship carrying passengers to Virginia or to a plantation, and had never been previously to Virginia. One passenger had died on the <u>Mayflower</u> and another when she arrived in the River of <u>Virginia</u>.

William Beadle of Limehouse, Middlesex, shipwright aged 50. He had fitted out a pinnace called the <u>George</u>, Mr. Matthew Graves, owned by Samuel Vassall, to accompany the <u>Mayflower</u> to Virginia.

William Williams of Limehouse, Middlesex, shipwright aged 30. Deposes as William Beadle.

Edmond Nailer of Wapping, Middlesex, shipwright aged 42. He has been a shipwright for 22 years and considered the <u>George</u> to be fit for a voyage to Virginia.

Matthew Graves of Limehouse, Middlesex, shipwright aged 39. He helped to fit out the <u>George</u>.

Richard Burton of Poplar, Middlesex, shipwright aged 60. He has been a shipwright for 40 years and helped refit the 25 ton pinnace <u>George</u> for her voyage to Virginia.

John Houghton of St. Dunstan in the East, London, fishmonger aged 60. In August 1633 he provisioned the <u>Mayflower</u> with fish.

Peter Holman of Limehouse, Middlesex, sailor aged 19. He has made 6 voyages to Virginia under Peter Andrewes and on the last waited upon him in his cabin. On that voyage one passenger died on passage and two more on the ship's arrival in Virginia, one at Little Town and one at James Town. On his other voyages to Virginia 3 or 4 passengers had died when there were not above 140 persons in the ship. While the <u>Mayflower</u> was at Martin's Hundred a Mr. Bell came aboard at Mr. Kingswell's order to collect those men aboard destined for Mr. Kingswell and Mr. Vassall.

Richard Johns of St. Ethelburga, Bishopsgate, London,

merchant aged 42. He sailed on the Mayflower from Gravesend in August 1633 and, when she was struck by bad weather in the Downs, went ashore at Deal. He shipped 21 passengers in her to Virginia for himself and his company. On passage to the Downs they were accompanied by the George pinnace, Mr. Stephen Champion, who declared that he would not continue to Virginia because his pinnace had proved so leaky. He was ordered back to London for repairs and told to follow on to Virginia later. The deponent has engaged in trade with Vassall and Andrewes for 4 or 5 years and has paid them £400 or £500 for freight of goods and passengers.

Peter Andrewes of Limehouse, Middlesex, mariner aged 39. In 1632 Samuel Vassall set out the pinnace George of London, Mr. Henry Taverner, for the discovery of the country of Carolana alias Florida, of a river navigable for shipping, and of a place suitable for a new plantation. In May or June 1633 the George returned to London and Taverner gave an account of his voyage to Vassall and Mr. Edward Kingswell. He reported the location of the entrance to the River of St. Helena and of two rivers adjoining, the depth of water in them, and the trade to be had with the Indians there. The Mayflower, being of 380 tons and drawing 16 feet of water when laden, was considered unsuitable by Mr. Taverner and Mr. Dunkyn to negotiate the entrance of the St. Helena River and Vassall offered Kingswell the choice of any other ship then in the Thames. A ship of 160 tons was found in St. Saviour's Dock but Kingswell insisted on having the Mayflower though Vassall maintained she would probably be cast away. Kingswell's resolve was to take a pinnace as an escort for the Mayflower and to ship his wife, whom he supposed to be with child, and his company, and on their arrival to send the pinnace on to Carolana to find a place where houses could be built in readiness for the following Spring. His intention was to spend the winter in Virginia with his wife and to follow on with her but in May 1634 both of them, with some others, returned from Virginia to London.

ENGLISH ADVENTURERS

Henry Taverner of All Hallows, Barking, London, mariner aged 32, deposes as Peter Andrewes. He returned from an exploration of the coast of Florida in July 1633 and reported to Mr. Kingswell at his lodgings in the Old Bailey. He was hired by Samuel Vassall to go as Master of the Thomas for a voyage to Virginia and Florida but 6 weeks were spent in waiting for passengers, then Vassall fell ill, and there followed further delays until May 1634 when, after Vassall had recovered somewhat, he employed a scrivener to write directions to be taken to his factor in Virginia, George Menefie, for Mr. Kingswell's company to be provided with what they needed for their voyage on to Florida. When the deponent arrived in Virginia in July 1634 he found that Kingswell had already left for London. He therefore took Vassall's instructions to Dr. Robotham and Mr. Cooke, kinsman and agent of Mr. Kingswell. The deponent remained 4 months in Virginia awaiting further orders from Kingswell but was then informed by Robotham that Kingswell would go to Florida direct from London.

Francis Agborowe of All Hallows, Barking, London, cooper aged 52. Henry Taverner is his son-in-law by marriage to his daughter. In May 1633 Taverner was Master of the Thomas of London and, by Samuel Vassall's order, was to embark passengers at Gravesend to be taken to Virginia and then to take 50 passengers from Virginia to a plantation at Florida belonging to Vassall.

Orpheus Dankin of Whitechapel, Middlesex, mariner aged 34. Samuel Vassall hired him in July 1633 to go as Master of his pinnace the Henry from London to Virginia and from thence to Florida in company with the Thomas, Mr. Henry Taverner. The Thomas departed from London two months before the Henry but both ships intended to go in company from Virginia to Florida. Before sailing from London the deponent went to Mr. Wingate, brother of Mr. Kingswell, to collect the malt which Wingate had promised to send to Virginia but was then told that the need had passed since Kingswell intended to come back to London. The deponent informed Wingate that several ships were then making ready in the Thames for Virginia including the Henry and those under Captain Felgate and Captain Douglas.   After he reached London Edward Kingswell said he intended to return to Virginia where he expected Samuel Vassall to provide a ship and pinnace to take his company from there.   In July 1633 Henry Taverner's wife and the wives of several seamen gave letters to the deponent to be delivered to their husbands in Virginia. He retained them until September 1633 when he set out in the Henry but, when she was being captured by the Biskayers, he threw the letters overboard so that her captors would not know her destination.

Daniel Jones of Ratcliffe, Middlesex, shipwright aged 24. He helped refit the pinnace George of London in Matthew Graves' quay in September 1633 and was persuaded by her Master, Stephen Champion, to go as her carpenter to Virginia to accompany the Mayflower. But off the Isle of Wight in stormy weather the George sprang a great leak and had to be left behind.

Thomas Willis of Limehouse, Middlesex, mariner aged 30. He was a quartermaster of the Mayflower. During her voyage to Virginia Margaret Dalton, maid to Mistress Wingate, was sick and was given additional beer to drink.   Peter Andrewes never gave her bad language though Mistress Wingate often gave Andrewes much scolding and taunting on the quarterdeck, such speeches as were not fit to give any man, much less to the commander of a ship.   The deponent heard Mistress Wingate tell other passengers they would do well to throw Andrewes overboard.

James Wilcockes of Limehouse, Middlesex, mariner aged 36. He was a quartermaster on the Mayflower and has made 3 other voyages on ships carrying passengers to St. Christopher's and one other on a ship carrying passengers to Virginia.

Robert Reeve of Ratcliffe, Middlesex, mariner aged 40. He was Master's Mate of the Mayflower and has made three other voyages to Virginia and one to St. Christopher's.

Clement East of Sonning, Berkshire, barber surgeon aged 42. As surgeon of the Mayflower he was able to call for fruit, sugar, spice and strong waters to treat the sick which was unusual on such ships unless passengers paid for such service over and above the cost of their passage of £6 per head. Mistress Wingate, Mr. Kingswell's sister, had spoken uncivilly to Peter Andrewes on a number of occasions.

Nicholas Agener of Ratcliffe, Middlesex, seaman aged 35. He was a steward on the Mayflower and has made 3 other voyages to Virginia in passenger ships.

Anne Gettings of Blackwall, Middlesex, widow aged 60. She went as a passenger in the Mayflower and returned in her to England. Since then she has been a passenger to Virginia in the Defence of London, Mr. Tobias Felgate, and returned home in the Thomas Bonadventure, Mr. Jeremy Blackman. Margaret Dalton who went outwards on the Mayflower with her was seasick and frequently stirred up and down the ship and used sometimes to lay with her in the gun room.

SIR DAVID KIRK v. JOHN DELABARR
THOMAS BREADCAKE v. SIR DAVID KIRK. 24 April to 4 December 1635.

Thomas Askewe of St. Saviour, Southwark, Surrey, sailor aged 50. He went as Mate of the Faith of London, Mr. Thomas Breadcake, on a voyage to Canada for which Sir David Kirk & Co. had appointed Captain Lewis Kirk as commander. The ship left Gravesend on 26 April 1634 in company with the St. George and the Caron to the Downs where Lewis Kirk joined the St. George. Off the Lizard they ran into a storm and were forced to return to Plymouth where Lewis Kirk resolved to abandon the enterprise. He sent his brother James Kirk to London who, after consulting Sir David Kirk, returned to Plymouth and ordered the Faith to

ENGLISH ADVENTURERS

Newfoundland to load fish on behalf of Mr. Delabarr. On her return voyage from Newfoundland she put into Spanish ports and at Barcelona in November 1634 the Marquesa de Villafranca, Lieutenant-General of Spanish Galleys, ordered the Faith's cables to be cut whereby she lost her tackle and ordnance.

Thomas Breadcake of Lee, Essex, sailor aged 43. He went as Master of the Faith and took fish aboard at Newfoundland. (Vol. 52).

John Breadcake, son of Thomas Breadcake, aged 20. He went as purser of the Faith.

Morgan Marrichurch of Mannerbere, Pembroke, navigator aged 23. He served as a common man on the Faith. (2 depositions in Vols. 51 & 52).

William Skinner of Burstow, Surrey, yeoman aged 28. He saw fish landed from the Faith at Cartagena. (Vol. 52).

Thomas Smyth of Redriffe, Surrey, mariner aged 42. He was employed as Master of the St. George for the voyage from London to Canada and from thence to Newfoundland and Spain. While the ship was at Newfoundland loading fish, Arthur Fountayne, Delabarr's factor there, was often drunk and distracted and had to be confined on board to prevent his running amok amongst the fishermen brandishing a naked sword.

Arthur Fountaine of St. Martin in the Fields, Midlesex, gent aged 28. He went to Canada as purser of the St. George, Mr. Thomas Smyth. (Vol. 52).

VOLUME 52

JOHN PRYNN v. ----- COUCHET. 25 June 1635.

Richard Ell examined for Couchet. He went as boatswain's mate on the Increase to Virginia where tobacco was loaded for the account of Captain John

Prynn. The deponent informed Mr. Stagg, Prynn's factor in Virginia, and Daniel Butcher, his marine, of what had been loaded from the tobacco packed in Mr. Hareward's house in Virginia. Stagg made James the cooper cut out marks from some of the hogsheads which had been delivered by one Major in Virginia and the deponent put his own mark on them to cancel a debt which Major owed him. Six passengers came home in the Increase, some of them gentlemen of good quality amongst whom were Sir John Zouch and his man and Captain Button. The deponent had hired Bartholomew Ellis, mariner, to serve in the ship and owed Prynn £6 for carrying one passenger to Virginia.

----- FLETCHER v. SIR JOHN LAWRENCE. 18 to 25 August 1635.

Nicholas Woodcocke of Wapping, Middlesex, sailor aged 50. He was Master of the Revenge of London which in May 1635 loaded tobacco, skins and other goods in Virginia from Richard Bennett to be delivered in London to Edward Bennett, John Stoner, Jonas Hopkins, Sir John Lawrence, William Penryn, Edward Robins, Ambrose Harmer and Nicholas Rainebird.

Edward Bennett of St. Olave, Hart Street, London, merchant aged 55, kinsman of Sir John Lawrence. In 1634 John Prynn adventured goods to Virginia which he consigned to Richard Bennett there. The deponent, Thomas Edwards, John Stoner and George Orme as partners had also sent goods to Richard Bennett by the Anne and Elizabeth on which Orme made the return voyage to Virginia. Anthony Edwards had received tobacco in London on behalf of Thomas Edwards.

ROBERT ANDERSON v. JOHN GIBBS. 22 to 25 August 1635.

James Bensly of Southampton, sailor aged 40. He went as gunner's mate on the Truelove, Mr. John Gibbs, which was chartered from London to New England and

Newfoundland and to return to the Straits. Robert Anderson, John Jenkins and Alexander Robinson were members of the crew and the latter two were often drunk and quarrelsome.

Nicholas Godfrey of Freshwater, Isle of Wight, sailor aged 46. He served as a common man in the Truelove.

Robert Bray of Plymouth, Devon, sailor aged 26. He was boatswain's mate of the Truelove.

EDWARD WIGGE v. THOMAS MIDDLETON. 21 October to 7 November 1635.

William Wigge of St. Benet Sherehog, London, but born at Milton Ernest, Bedfordshire, grocer aged 36. He has known the defendant Middleton since the beginning of the voyage of the Robert Bonadventure which loaded tobacco in Virginia consigned to London by the deponent's brother there, Edward Wigge. When the ship arrived back in Dover one of her owners, Thomas Browne, asked the deponent to agree to send the tobacco by the same ship to Holland but he refused and asked for it to be forwarded to London, as Thomas Middleton had since confessed to Captain Langham, Samuel Vassall and Maurice Thompson. Nevertheless the ship proceeded to Holland where she was seized and taken to Dunkirk. The deponent was owed 4000 weight of tobacco by his brother Edward Wigge.

Gabriel Kinge, apprentice to William Wigge, born in Lombard Street, London, aged 18. His sister is married to William Wigge and he has known Edward Wigge for 3 years. Thomas Browne, one of the owners of the Robert Bonadventure, brought a letter from Edward Wigge to William Wigge's shop in Bucklersbury, London, and in March 1634/5 William Wigge paid Francis Gaurney for Virginia tobacco.

Humphrey Farley of St. Stephen Walbrook, London, but born in the City or Worcester, grocer aged 41. He went to Gravesend to prepare accounts for the Robert

<u>Bonadventure</u> on her outward voyage. In April 1635, before news of the ship's capture by the Dunkirkers had arrived, Wigge told him at the Three Cranes Tavern in the Poultry that he had contracted for his tobacco to go to Holland. The deponent is a trader in Virginia tobacco.

William Wigge of St. Benet Sherehog, London, grocer aged 37. (2nd deposition). In May 1635 the differences between Edward Wigge and Thomas Middleton over the prices paid for Virginia tobacco were referred for arbitration to Captain Langham and Samuel Vassall.

THOMAS MOORE & JOHN DIGBY v. JOHN THIERRY.
15 December 1635 to 3 July 1637.

Henry Williamson of St. Dunstan in the East, London, upholsterer (draper) aged 25 (26). (2 depositions). In October 1635 Thomas Moore arranged with John Thierry for the transportation of himself and his servants William Kinge and John Mutchell to Virginia on the <u>Constance</u> which he was informed was as well found and victualled as any ship which went there. He agreed on a price of £6 per head payable at Gravesend. The ship failed to make the voyage because of which Moore's servants were left behind in England and Thierry refused to refund the passage money. The deponent was a witness to the payment to Thierry of £40 at the Christopher Inn in Gravesend by Richard Rudderford, planter in Virginia, for the passage of himself and 7 servants.

John Withins of St. Andrew, Holborn, London, gent aged 26. He booked his passage to Virginia in the <u>Constance</u> of London of which John Thierry, merchant of London, was part owner. After the ship left Gravesend she was stayed in the Downs for 2 weeks by contrary winds, victuals ran short, and there were so many passengers that many, including the deponent, were forced on to the bare decks. When they could obtain no redress many passengers threatened to go ashore and the deponent's wife secured his release by hiring another man to go in his place. While still off the Downs the Constance sprang a great leak and the seamen threatened they would not continue their voyage if they could get away. The deponent left the ship before she reached Dover and has since seen Moore's two servants in London.

John Ashcroft of St. Andrew, Holborn, London, embroiderer aged 32. He had booked his passage in the Constance in which the passengers were so short of beer that some drank salt water to slake their thirst. His master Mr. Christopher Boyes, Captain Dawson, Mr. Rotherford and Mr. Dodd who were also bound to Virginia with their servants complained about the conditions on board, and when the ship put into Dover several passengers escaped including Thomas Moore and his servants.

John Bradstreet of St. Peter ad Vincula in the Tower of London, tallow chandler aged 31. He was present at the Christopher Tavern in Gravesend in October 1635 when Henry Williamson, who dwelt in Thames Street, London, paid Thierry £19 in passage money.

John Smyth of St. Katherine by the Tower, London, hosier aged 40. In October 1635 he lodged Thomas Hudson who was to go passenger in the Constance to Virginia.

Thomas Palmer of St. Giles Cripplegate, London, merchant tailor aged 34. (2 depositions). In October 1635 he went to Gravesend to see a child and servant of his shipped in the Constance. While there he saw Edmond Porter, soapboiler of St. Botolph, Aldersgate, London, pay Thierry £36 for the passage to Virginia of himself and 5 servants.

Marjery Jackson, wife of James Jackson of Ratcliffe, Middlesex, distiller, aged 50. In October 1635 at the request of her kinsman Francis Bristowe she delivered to (Clement) Champion, Master of the Constance, strong waters to the value of £18 to pay for the passage to Virginia of Bristowe and his 2 servants

William Gillam and John Gretwood. They were put ashore in the West Country because of which Bristowe was obliged to make over his own and his 2 servants' places to Christopher Boyes, a planter in Virginia, who was a passenger on the same ship.

Henry Morrell, servant to Captain Charles Dawson of Flushing in Zealand, aged 19. On 21 October 1635 Dawson paid Thierry £12 at Gravesend for his own and the deponent's passage. All the passengers were landed at Ilfracombe, Devon, where the deponent and others stayed for 3 months until the ship's voyage was quite given up.

George Taylor of Christchurch, London, mercer aged 39. He was a passenger in the Constance, whose purser, Jeffrey Gough, informed him that the ship was forced to put into Ilfracombe in January 1635/6 because of her leakiness. The purser paid him, Captain Charles Dawson, Richard Rotherford, Edmond Porter, Walter Jenkins, Christopher Boyes and others an allowance for their diet while they were ashore.

Richard Preice of St. Mary Rowe, London, scrivener aged 29. In October 1635 he was at the dwelling in St. Botolph, Aldgate, of John Smyth, citizen and draper of London, and on his behalf took £12 to John Thierry's house in Turnwheel Lane to pay for the passage to Virginia of John Cooke and Henry Johnson.

John Bourne, apprentice of Thomas Palmer of St. Giles Cripplegate, London, merchant tailor. He saw his master deliver strong waters to Thierry to pay for the passage to Virginia of Palmer's son and a servant.

Christopher Boyes of Virginia, planter aged 36. At Hartle Rowe in Hampshire he arranged with Jeffery Gough, purser of the Constance, for the passage to Virginia of his servants William Gillam, John Elwoode, Thomas Hudson and William Hulett. The deponent also arranged the passage of 2 others who were not his servants, one Baskerfield and John Saddocke.

ENGLISH ADVENTURERS

Edmond Porter of St. Botolph, Aldersgate, London, draper aged 36. He, Richard Rudderforde and Walter Jenkins received from the ship's purser £4 which they promised to repay in tobacco at Virginia. The deponent had 5 servants of his own on the ship and 2 others were handed over to him, Griffith ?Manner and John Palmer, servants of (Thomas) Palmer. He also received from the purser money to pay for the diet of 38 passengers on the <u>Constance</u>.

Walter Jenkins of St. Margaret, Westminster, Middlesex, planter aged 35. He had undertaken to pay the ship's purser in tobacco at Virginia the passage money for 6 of his servants.

Charles Dawson of Flushing, Zealand, Esq aged 42. He arranged for the passage to Virginia of his own servant Henry Morrell and for Mr. Harwood's servant, John Saddocke.

Richard Rudderforde of Virginia, planter aged 40. He embarked 7 men and women servants of his on the <u>Constance</u>.

John Digby of St. Andrew Hubbard, London, citizen and pewterer of London aged 44. He hired a passage on the ship for Sampson Alkin and for some goods for Virginia.

Praise Barbone of St. Bride, Fleet Street, London, leatherseller aged 38. (Vol. 53).

Stephen Moore of St. Andrew Hubbard, London, clothworker aged 23. (Vol. 53).

Thomas Venner of All Hallows, Barking, London, wine cooper aged 28. (Vol. 53).

Isaac Hartwell of St. Botolph, Billingsgate, London, waterman aged 50. (Vol. 53).

Richard Young of All Hallows Staining, London, cooper aged 37. (Vol. 53).

Robert Burgess of Colliton, Devon, merchant aged 42. (Vol. 53).

William Starbucke of Lambeth Marsh, Surrey, tailor aged 31. (Vol. 53).

Roger Fletcher of All Hallows Barking, London, sailor aged 34. (Vol. 53).

JOSEPH HAWES v. JOHN PAYNE.
HENRY FABIAN v. JOSEPH HAWES.
PHILIP WHITE v. JOHN BEALE. 23 January 1635/6 to 7 December 1638.

Hugh Bullock of All Hallows Barking, London, Esq aged 59, deposes for Robert Tokelye, Joseph Hawes and others. He is a Member of the State of Virginia and came home as a passenger in the John and Dorothy, Mr. Thomas Burley, who had given a bond to the Custom House in London to bring his ship back to London. But contrary to Burley's wishes, the ship's Captain, John Payne, had ordered her into Galloway, Ireland, on her return from Virginia.

Christopher Boyes of Blunt Point, Virginia, gent aged 38. He returned from Virginia in the John and Dorothy and understood from a conversation with Thomas Burley that he would be imprisoned if his ship did not return to England as was required by his bond.

Samuel Leigh of Wapping, Middlesex, mariner aged 37. (2 depositions: aged 39 in April 1637). In May 1635 Captain John Payne commanded the John and Dorothy to be taken into Galloway despite objections from the deponent, Captain (Hugh) Bullock, Christopher Boyes and Abraham English, the chiefest passengers. Once in Galloway, Payne rode to Dublin where he sold tobacco to one Weale though he confessed he had received no orders to go to Ireland. (Vols. 53 & 54).

Thomas Burley of Redriffe, Surrey, mariner aged 52/53. (2 depositions). Joseph Hawes' factor on the ship was

ENGLISH ADVENTURERS

James Homewood and John Payne had received instructions not to meddle with Hawes' goods on board. (Vols. 52 & 53). The ship was sold in Galway and then freighted to Edward Rochford for a voyage to Limerick before being cast away on the Isle of Wight.

Thomas Taylor of Bristol, merchant aged 55. He loaded tobacco for himself and Christopher Carew of Bristol in the John and Dorothy in January 1634/5 while she was at anchor in James River, Virginia. In June 1636 he went to Galway where he believed the ship had been for some time and, after litigation, obtained possession of his tobacco, much of which was by then rotten. (Vol. 53).

Richard Knevitt of Holy Trinity, Minories, London, mariner. Burley obtained a warrant to sell his ship at Galway. (Vol. 53).

James Homewood of Dover, Kent, seaman aged 40. He was purser of the John and Dorothy. John Payne is now (July 1637) a prisoner in Dublin. (Vol. 53).

Edward Mullard of Stepney, Middlesex, armourer aged 42. He went in the ship to Virginia and she left Gravesend on 2 September 1634. (Vol. 53).

John Flood servant of John Beale, aged 19. In July 1634 John Payne sold a share in the ship to Beale and the deponent made the return voyage to Virginia in her as far as the Isle of Wight where she was cast away. (Vol. 53).

Valentine Mumford of Ratcliffe, Middlesex, sailor aged 39, deposes for Henry Fabian whom he has known for 8 years. Joseph Hawes owned the John and Dorothy on which the deponent went as gunner from London to Virginia while Henry Fabian was Master's mate. She left Gravesend in September 1634 carrying freight and passengers and the deponent fired 3 pieces of ordnance on her departure. At Virginia Fabian left the ship to join another as Master. On the return voyage, while the John and Dorothy was at Galloway, Ireland, one of her quartermasters, Walter Hancocke, was discharged. (Vol. 54).

Thomas Burley of Redriffe, Surrey, sailor aged 52. (3rd deposition). Joseph Hawes owned half of the John and Dorothy and employed the deponent as Master. In Virginia Henry Fabian was appointed to go as Master of a Flemish ship. Walter Hancock who was discharged was a contentious fellow. (Vol. 54).

Benjamin Bowden of Stepney, Middlesex, sailor aged 37. He has made 4 voyages to Virginia and back, 2 as Master's mate and 2 as a Master. (Vol. 54).

Robert Shapton of Limehouse, Middlesex, sailor aged 38. He has been a Master of ships for 6 years and has made several voyages to Virginia, Barbados and the West Indies. (Vol. 54).

UNNAMED SUIT. 1 to 4 February 1635/6.

Thomas Kirk of St. Mary Axe, London, Esq aged 30. He was chief commander of the Fort at Quebec in Canada when it was burned down but at that time was at Three Rivers, 30 miles away. The fire was caused by eels hung up to dry in the kitchen which fell into the fire. Some 8 days after he had received orders from the King he surrendered the Fort to the French and ever since that time has refrained from trading there.

Lewis Tucker of Wapping, Middlesex, mariner aged 28. He was at Quebec at the time of the fire.

John le Bailly of Amiens, Picardy, aged 34. He was at Quebec at the time of the fire.

WILLIAM GREENE v. VINCENT DELABARR. 10 February 1635/6 to 20 May 1636.

Thomas Palmer of St. Dunstan in the East, London, citizen and mercer of London aged 48. He has known

William Greene for 10 years and Vincent Delabarr for 9. He was a landwaiter at the Custom House, London, and on 29 March 1633 entered the <u>Little Anne</u> of London, Mr. Robert Dennis, as having come from Virginia.

Robert Dennis of Limehouse, Middlesex, sailor aged 33. The <u>Little Anne</u> was freighted by Vincent Delabarr and John Stoner from 1 January 1631/2 to 15 April 1633 for a voyage from London to Virginia or St. Christopher's and return.

William Bradford of Limehouse, Middlesex, sailor aged 30. He went as carpenter in the ship.

HENRY FETHERSTON & THOMAS BABB v. THOMAS SANTLEY. 16 March 1635/6 to 15 June 1636.

Thomas Beale of Colchester, Essex, sailor aged 48. He was a quartermaster of the <u>Hopewell</u> in which Thomas Santley loaded goods in London to be delivered to New England and Virginia. She arrived off Plymouth, New England, in November 1635 when the pilot taken on board to guide her into harbour ran her aground and weakened her to such an extent that her Master, Richard French, gave her up for lost and told Thomas Babb to save what he could. Her passengers for Virginia had to be sent in other ships. It was a time of year in those parts when the winds blow westerly for 3 or 4 months together until February, and so much is generally observed by the seamen that go thither: it is a contrary wind for Virginia but a good one for England. A voyage from New England to Virginia may be made in a fortnight with a favourable wind but, without one, may take a quarter of a year. There was nowhere in those parts of New England to bring a ship ashore to be repaired, though materials were available. French decided, therefore, to take the <u>Hopewell</u> back to London rather than proceed to his original plan, particularly as she had proved leaky on the outward voyage and none of the passengers had been able to keep dry in their cabins.

ENGLISH ADVENTURERS

Jeremiah Lampin of Ratcliffe, Middlesex, sailor aged 40. He was hired by Thomas Babb to go as Master's mate of the <u>Hopewell</u> and on her outward passage 11 or 12 passengers were intended to go from New England to Virginia. Goods loaded in London by Thomas Santley were safely discharged at Boston and the ship arrived back in London on 14 February 1635/6. John Pearse also shipped goods in London to be delivered to one Cane in New England. Ships are not built at Plymouth, New England, but 12 leagues away at Boston.

John Herringman of Limehouse, Middlesex, sailor aged 24. He went as carpenter of the <u>Hopewell</u>. By the report of the inhabitants there, the pilot taken aboard at Plymouth, a man named Watson, had sailed the New England coast for 5 or 6 years and was an able man. There are many flats and shoals on the passage from New England to Virginia.

Erasmus Studd of Wapping, Middlesex, navigator aged 23. Mr. Bentley, a passenger in the gun room, had 10 servants on board to be delivered to Virginia who were obliged to leave the ship in New England and go on by other vessels. In New England there are trees growing sufficient to furnish a ship with planks and timber for repairs but nowhere near where the <u>Hopewell</u> ran aground was there a place to bring her ashore.

RICHARD ORCHARD v. LORD BALTIMORE. 9 May to 15 June 1636.

Sir John Harvye, Governor of His Majesty's Colony in Virginia, aged 54. In November 1634 Leonard Calvert and Mr. Jerome Hawlye, owners of the pinnace <u>Dove</u>, came to him with a complaint against her Master, Richard Orchard, for leaving his ship at risk and for behaving insolently. Orchard and his men had refused to return to their ship unless their outstanding wages were paid, and Calvert and Hawlye refused to make payment unless or until the pinnace returned to Maryland.

John Games of Ratcliffe, Middlesex, sailor aged 34. He was hired by Orchard in 1631 together with Samuel Lawson, Richard Kenton, John Curle, and Nicholas Perry to serve in the Dove for a voyage from London to the West Indies and Virginia. Calvert and Baltimore had asked Orchard to take one boy free to Virginia but promised to pay the passage of a cabin boy. Calvert had threatened to hang Orchard if he would not take the pinnace from Virginia to Maryland. In June 1634 Leonard Calvert, Captain Hawlye and Captain Cornwallis sent the Dove with corn from Maryland to Mathew Tewses (sic) Bay in New England and, on the way, she stayed at Virginia to take on a pilot and have her bottom refurbished. Returning from New England she was forced by contrary winds to put into Point Comfort, Virginia, and, understanding that Calvert and Hawlye were then in Virginia, Orchard went to demand wages from them.

Richard Kempton of Tower Wharf, London, sailor aged 24. He was hired as boatswain of the Dove and Nicholas Perry was hired as a sailor. Lord Baltimore, Leonard Calvert, Jeremy Hawley and Thomas Cornwallis had fitted out the pinnace for service in Maryland and in 1633 she was to accompany the Arke and her passengers from Gravesend to Maryland but, on passage, the two vessels separated and did not meet again until they reached the West Indies. Captain Curle died before the pinnace reached Virginia. After the crew had served for 13 months they demanded their wages from Calvert, then in Virginia, and were told that they would be paid in Maryland or not at all. In January 1633/4 the ships sailed in company from Barbados to Montserrat and St. Christopher's and later in 1634 Orchard set out from Maryland in the Dove to Hackamacke in Virginia, victualled there, and went on to New England to deliver corn. He then intended to return to Maryland but was taken short of wind and forced to put back into Virginia.

Nicholas Perry of Jernematha (sic), Isle of Wight, sailor aged 26. He went as quartermaster of the Dove.

DAVID DAVIDSON, AUGUSTINE ALDRIDGE, RANDALL MAINWARING & NATHANIEL HAWES v. JOHN THIERRY. 14 February 1636/7 to 28 November 1637.

Martin Aldridge, natural son of Augustine Aldridge, aged 17. In 1635 John Thierry came to his father's house in Wapping to arrange for his ship the <u>Safety</u> to be fitted for a voyage to Virginia. While the ship was in the yard her Master was John Grant and William Martyn kept an account of the work done on her.

Edward Robins of St. Dunstan in the East, London, previously of St. Mary Magdalene, Milk Street, London, but born at Buckby, Northants, merchant aged 34. When the <u>Safety</u> returned from Virginia, Mainwaring went on board her in the Thames and ordered her Master, Timothy Winge, to leave her. The deponent was paid by William Anthony for freighting the ship to Virginia.

John Digby of St. Andrew Hubbard, London, where he has lived for 10 years, but born at Grundan, Northants, citizen and pewterer of London and a trader in tobacco, aged 40. When the <u>Safety</u> was delivered up to Mainwaring there were two pigs aboard.

John Thierry of St. Mary Bothaw, London, merchant aged 34. He had purchased the <u>Safety</u>, formerly the <u>St. Cloud</u>. His brother James Thierry became bound on his behalf to Bartholomew Nicholls of Plymouth, merchant, and the deponent then made over the <u>Safety</u> to his brother and she was sold to Nathaniel Hawes. The deponent had been in prison as a bankrupt and the ship was never in fact in James Thierry's possession since he was not in England.

Stephen Thompson, apprentice to Gilbert Stonechest, born at Needham, Suffolk, aged 21. The <u>Safety</u> was fitted with masts taken from the <u>Bonny Bess</u> of which John Thierry was the owner.

Grace Winge, wife of Timothy Winge of St. Botolph, Aldgate, London, aged 27. She went to Gravesend to take leave of her husband when he went as Master of the Safety to Virginia.

Thomas Combes, servant of Anthony Freer, aged 18. John Thierry was the owner of the Safety which was freighted by John Grant and others.

Charles Greene, servant of David Davidson, aged 19. His master had sent goods by the Safety to Virginia.

Richard Bendlowe, servant of Nathaniel Hawes, aged 22. In June 1634 his master had sent goods to John Thierry to be freighted to Virginia.

Robert Offley, servant of Nathaniel Hawes, aged 24. John Thierry made over the Safety to Randall Mainwaring to settle a debt.

Thomas Lovett, servant of Randall Mainwaring, aged 24. William Anthony paid his master for the freight of the Safety.

CHRISTOPHER VENNARD & WILLIAM JONES v. LORD VANE.
SAMUEL & PETER FORTRY v. RICHARD GURLING.
17 February 1636/7 to 28 November 1638.

Christopher Vennard of Ratcliffe, Middlesex, mariner aged 36, deposes for Abigail Vennard, widow. (2 depositions). Richard Gurling was Master of the Hope of Ipswich from June 1634 until his death on 14 May 1636 when he was succeeded by the deponent. The ship sailed from Harwich but, meeting a violent storm off Woodbridge, was forced to return to Ipswich for repairs where Gurling declared his intention of sailing for Boston, New England, and then to the Isle of May for salt which he would take to Ostend. But they missed the Isle of May and went instead to the West Indies where Gurling died. Bartholomew Sterne who had been hired as a carpenter was lost in a pinnace in

Barbados in February 1634/5. The ship returned to London on 15 September 1636.

Thomas Warner of Harwich, Essex, cooper aged 62. His apprentice, Peter Bond, was hired by Gurling to go on the voyage.

Robert Casson of Ipswich, Suffolk, mariner. His son Samuel Casson was hired for the voyage but received no wages.

Richard Sheppard of Brixton, Devon, aged 58. He was hired at Plymouth as the ship's cook.

Robert Anderson of Wapping, Middlesex, mariner aged 34. He went as Master of the Hope, which was owned by Edmond Cason, with a cargo of salt but in January 1636/7 met with a violent storm and put into a Dutch plantation on the Hudson River in New England. There the ice turned her on her side and she had to be abandoned.

John Emans of St. Benet Finck, London, notary puiblic aged 57.

Nicholas Jacobson of St. Botolph, Aldgate, London, sailmaker aged 54. He supplied canvas for the Hope.

Robert Lea of St. Andrew Wardrobe, London, merchant aged 24. He went as purser of the Hope but left her at Barbados. Her passengers were carried to New England.

Richard Parr, servant of William Jones, aged 28. In February or March 1634/5 his master sent Gurling goods with which to fit out the Hope but Gurling wrote to him from Ipswich asking for payment to be deferred until the ship returned from New England. Henry Hatsell, former servant of William Jones, had recovered some money on behalf of Abigail Vennard.

Joanna Hopkins, wife of Jeffrey Hopkins of Ratcliffe, Middlesex, sailor, aged 55. In June 1638 her husband went to New England as boatswain of the Hope, Mr. Richard Gurling. (Vol. 54).

Jeffery Hopkins of Ratcliffe, Middlesex, sailor aged 56. Deposes as above. (Vol. 54).

Thomas Peach of Ipswich, Suffolk, sailor aged 40. While the Hope was at Ipswich he agreed that Vennard should go as his mate to New England. (Vol. 54).

John Keyes of Ratcliffe, Middlesex, sailor aged 57. In June 1634 Thomas Peach who was Master of a ship employed Christopher Vennard to serve as Master's mate on the Hope for a voyage from Harwich to New England. After being in New England, Vennard and his servants Rowland Davies and Edward Clemens returned in the ship to London. (Vol. 54).

Rowland Davies of Ratcliffe, Middlesex, sailor aged 25. He went boatswain's mate on the Hope. Edward Clemence, since deceased, joined the ship at Ipswich as apprentice to Vennard. On the voyage to New England Richard Gurling died. (Vol. 54).

Simon Peters of Wapping, Middlesex, sailor aged 26. He was an apprentice to Richard Gurling whom he served on a voyage from London to the East Land and Dunkirk and back to Ipswich, and afterwards served with him on the voyage to New England and Barbados. After Gurling's death, Christopher Venner was Master for the voyage from Barbados to London. (Vol. 54).

Robert Sarah of Shadwell, Middlesex, navigator aged 25. (2 depositions). He shipped in the Hope when she called at Plymouth on her way to New England and served as her quartermaster. She left Barbados for London at the end of August 1636.
(Vols. 53 & 54).
- See also **ONIONS v. THE HOPE**, p.....

----- **PERRY v. WILLIAM PENRYN.**
WILLIAM DOUGLAS v. FRANCIS SMITH. 17 April

ENGLISH ADVENTURERS

1637 to 7 March 1637/8.

Isaac Watlington of St. Mary at Hill, London, mariner aged 36 (38). (2 depositions). He went as Master of the <u>Damask Rose</u> from London to Virginia and took William Penryn aboard as a passenger at the Isle of Wight. Penryn died on 24 November 1636 and was buried at sea.

John Fleming of St. Michael, Crooked Lane, London, servant of George Plummer, surgeon aged 18. He went as surgeon of the <u>Damask Rose</u>. William Penryn, who was a churchwarden in the parish where the deponent lived, joined the ship at the Isle of Wight on 24 August 1636 but died off the coast of Virginia.

Richard Bland of Stratford by Bow, Essex, servant of Captain William Douglas, aged 22. He was resident in Virginia when, a little before Christmas 1636, Francis Smith came there and showed him a letter of attorney from Captain Douglas authorising Smith to receive his money and tobacco in Virginia. These were shipped on the <u>Damask Rose</u> on which the deponent returned to England.

GILBERT HOUGH v. EDWARD TASKER.
EDWARD TASKER, JOHN LAKE & HUMPHREY CUNDYE v. HENRY MADDISON & WILLIAM DAWSON.
18 April 1637 to 23 February 1637/8.

Thomas Miller of Ratcliffe, Middlesex, sailor aged 41. He went as Master's mate of the <u>Little Neptune</u>, Mr. Edward Barnes, on a voyage from London to New England, returning to London by way of the Canary Islands. The ship's owners were Tasker, Lake and Cundye, who altered and provisioned her for the voyage but the provisions supplied by Gilbert Hough were unfit. The deponent paid William Stevens, a carpenter of Marblehead, New England, for work he carried out on the ship. John Daniel succeeded Edward Barnes as her Master.

ENGLISH ADVENTURERS

Alexander Howe of Horsey Down, Surrey, sailor aged 35. He was a quartermaster of the ship.

Stephen Boulton of Wapping, Middlesex, sailor aged 50. He was also a quartermaster.

Thomas Pope of Wapping, Middlesex, sailmaker aged 45. He provided sails for the <u>Little Neptune</u>.

Samuel West of St. Saviour, Southwark, Surrey, salter aged 31. In March 1633/4 he delivered salt to Thomas Miller of the <u>Little Neptune</u>.

Richard Atherall of Horsey Down, Surrey, rope maker aged 47. He delivered cable to the ship.

John Tappan of St. Olave, Southwark, Surrey, brewer aged 30. He delivered beer to the ship for which payment was made to Mrs. Knight now in New England.

James Moore of Wapping, Middlesex, pulley maker aged 23. His master William Transcombe of Wapping, now deceased, delivered goods to the ship.

Giles Foster of St. Saviour, Southwark, Surrey, butcher aged 50. He supplied beef to the ship.

Henry Nicholls of St. Olave, Southwark, Surrey, sawyer aged 29. He provided timber for repairs to the ship.

Randall Ellis, servant and book-keeper of John Lake, aged 25. He was responsible for paying for the ship's provisions. John Daniel bought fodder in Weymouth and Dorchester for the cattle being carried to New England in the <u>Little Neptune</u>.

John Daniel of Redriffe, Surrey, sailor aged 26. In March 1633/4 he was appointed by Tasker & Co. to go as Master of the <u>Little Neptune</u> to New England and to return by way of the Canaries. Her owners were to have £8 per head to transport 48 cattle to New England but 13 died before reaching there.

ENGLISH ADVENTURERS

RE THE DAVID OF LONDON. 21 April 1637.

Robert Armitage of St. Martin Orgars, London, merchant aged 36. He supplied goods to John Powick alias Grister to be shipped in the David to Virginia.

Nicholas Copley of St. Nicholas Acons, London, merchant tailor aged 34. He also supplied goods to be shipped.

RE THE ELIZABETH OF LONDON. 27 April 1637.

Thomas Yonge, residing at the house of John Farrington, merchant, in Lothbury, London, mariner aged 50. He was Master of the Elizabeth which became dangerously leaky as she was coming from Charles River to Delaware Bay in June 1635. When she arrived at Point Comfort, Virginia, her company refused to proceed further and Thomas Stagge, factor for the owners, offered to pay them off in tobacco. In 1636 when the deponent was in Virginia he saw in Stagge's account books a note of a payment made to the ship's carpenter, Edward Bateman.

RE THE REBECCA OF LONDON. 11 to 13 May 1637.

Andrew Johnson of Wapping, Middlesex, sailor aged 56. He went as gunner of the Rebecca, Mr. Richard Buckham, on a voyage from Gravesend to Virginia during which Francis Drake, the gunner's mate, fell sick, was put ashore in Virginia and died there after 10 weeks. The Master's mate, Peter Rexford alias Richartes, was believed to have kicked Drake and broken his thigh.

Anthony Bluett, servant of Richard Buckham, of Limehouse, Middlesex, aged 18.

Richard Gribble, dwelling at King Street near Gravel Lane, Wapping Wall, Middlesex, aged 50.

Thomas Hodges of Limehouse, Middlesex, surgeon aged

23. He set Drake's thigh in Virginia.

HENRY HUTCHINSON v. RICHARD BENNETT, ANTHONY JONES & ROBERT SABINE. 26 June 1637 to 13 November 1639.

John Rosier of Warwicks Squeak, Virginia, clerk aged 34. He buried William Hutchinson who died 3/4 years ago leaving a will of which Richard Bennett is the overseer. After his death the father, Henry Hutchinson, came to Virginia to collect his son's assets but died there. The Governor of Virginia then appointed Thomas Burbage to take account of the estate and sell it. The defendants had obtained nothing from the estate but trouble.

James Stone, living at the house of Thomas Freer in Thames Street, London, merchant aged 26. William Hutchinson's will is on record in the Court of Virginia. The father Henry Hutchinson died 12 months after the son William Hutchinson. The deponent went to Virginia after the father's death since both father and son were indebted to him. William Hutchinson was generally accounted a rich man having a plantation, cattle and servants in Virginia.

George Putt of Limehouse, Middlesex, mariner aged 29. While the John and Barbara on which he served was at Hog Island, Virginia, Anthony Jones, a planter, came aboard to receive and Admiralty Commission which was enclosed in a black leather box. After he had broken the seals Jones told the deponent it had arrived too late. The deponent understood that Jones had been sent over to Virginia to receive the Hutchinsons' estate but had not received notice until too late of a sitting of the Quarter Court. The John and Barbara had been 4 months on passage from London to Virginia. (Vol.54).

Edward Harris of St. Dunstan in the East, London, merchant aged 41. In February or March 1637/8 he stood surety for Richard Bennett on behalf of Henry Hutchinson in an Admiralty cause. Bennett had written him a letter dated Point Comfort, Virginia, 6 January

1637/8 intimating that Mr. Robert Sabyn had sent him a Commission dated about December 1637. (Vol. 54).

Robert Sabyn of Maides Mill, Herts, tallow chandler aged 45. An Admiralty Commission in the cause of Hutchinson & Co. v. Richard Bennett, Anthony Jones and Robert Sabyn which was instituted in August 1637 was sent to Virginia by the John and Barbara, Mr. John Barker, for the examination of witnesses in Virginia on behalf of the defendants. It was to have been delivered to Bennett or Jones at Warwicks Quicke, Virginia. (Vol. 54).

Allen Kennistone of Warwick Squeak, Virginia, planter aged 40. He has lived in Virginia for 17 years and was a near neighbour of William Hutchinson. The custom there is that those who hold goods belonging to a deceased person are summoned before the Governor and Council to give an account of them before being obliged to surrender goods, or services for them, to the administrator of the deceased. The deponent has himself been an administrator in Virginia. On the death of William Hutchinson, the Governor appointed the father Henry Hutchinson to act as administrator and required Anthony Jones, Richard Bennett and Robert Fabian to account for the debts they owed to the estate. Henry Hutchinson then died suddenly and the Court granted administration to Thomas Burbage for the use of those who had rights in the estate. When he died William Hutchinson owned a plantation, servants and cattle. (Vol. 55).

Nicholas Spackman, late of Warwick Squeak, Virginia, now citizen and vintner of London, aged 49. He was Court prosecutor in Virginia and was present when Jones, Bennett and Fabian were called to account. (Vol. 55).

Edward Major of Nants Mum alias the Upper County of New Norfolk, Virginia, gent aged 26. He was employed as a Burgess in the Virginia Court. When an administrator there has made satisfaction to the Court he is discharged from any other claim and this custom has been observed for more than 5 years during which time he has been an administrator there himself. (Vol. 55).

Robert Davis of Warwick Squeak, Virginia, planter aged 36. He has lived in Virginia for more than 20 years and has often appraised the goods of deceased persons. He was present when William Hutchinson chose his executors. (Vol. 55).

ROGER PHILLIPS v. WILLIAM WHITE.
----- COBHAM & ----- COBHAM v. JOHN BIGGE & THOMAS BESBECH. 14 July 1637 to 31 January 1637/8.

John Cobham of Rochester, Kent, aged 34. William White purchased the Blessing of Rochester and paid off the debts which she had incurred from her last voyage to New England.

John Jobson of Rochester, Kent, sailor aged 42. He was Master of the Blessing owned by Bigge and Besbech and she was in debt for equipment and provisions supplied for her last voyage to New England. On her return she was arrested by Mr. Bulteel.

PHILIP LUXON/LUXTON v. WILLIAM HARRIS & NICHOLAS JOLLYE. 24 & 25 July 1637.

Philip Callow of Bristol, cooper aged 20. He joined the Blessing of Falmouth, Mr. Philip Luxon, at Padstow, Cornwall, for a voyage to Virginia as her steward. While she was at James Town he forbade the Master to break open cases on board but despite this he opened and consumed a case of strong waters and forced the deponent to drink with him. It was discovered that the crew had cut a way into the ship's hold to get at the drink. On the return voyage some of her company deserted at Kinsale, Ireland, and at Falmouth thereby causing her tobacco to be neglected and spoiled.

Walter Childes of Bristol, clothworker aged 29. He went as a passenger on the Blessing to assist the purser Henry Tatton to sell William Harris's goods in Virginia and saw Luxon go to the hold before a case of strong waters and other goods were found open or missing. Luxon arranged for a lock to be put on his cabin and did not allow planters to enter it, and for that reason several refused to trade their tobacco with him. The ship's company numbered 14 and she carried 2 or 3 passengers. James Sherland was her mate, John Marten and Philip Callow stewards. She remained in Virginia for 14 weeks and, on her return to England, her tobacco was found to be damaged by rot.

Henry Tatton of Bristol, servant of William Harris, aged 21. The ship's carpenter broke into the hold with her Master's consent.

HUGH WESTON, SIMON HACKE, JOHN CASTLE, THOMAS LEDDOZE, THOMAS MACE, HENRY HEADLY, GREGORY CLEMENTS, ANTHONY SLATER, AMBROSE HARMER & RICHARD ORCHARD v. JOSEPH SAUNDERS.
JOSEPH SAUNDERS v. MAURICE THOMPSON, RICHARD ORCHARD & HUGH WESTON.
SAMUEL LEDDOZE v. GEORGE GRACE. 25 July 1637 to 2 March 1639/40.

Philip Dodsworth of Limehouse, Middlesex, merchant aged 30. He went to Virginia in the Flower de Luce, Mr. Hugh Weston and loaded tobacco for London on behalf of Henry Headly, Thomas Mace and William Bradshaw. On the outward voyage the ship proved leaky and in Virginia Weston broke open a chest of goods. Henry Headly sold some stockings to John Bell in Virginia.

William Blundestone of St. Katherine, Coleman Street, London, clothworker and apprentice to Mr. Sherstone, aged 19. Joseph Saunders adventured £2000 in the voyage but received only 2 hogsheads of tobacco on his own account. Weston had a very bad reputation for cutting out the marks of goods carried on his ship. If the Flower de Luce had not been pumped day and night on the return voyage she would have sunk.

Thomas Cobb of Wapping, Middlesex, ship carpenter aged 57. He, Robert Tranchmore who was a master shipwright, and Augustine Aldridge, shipwright, had viewed the Flower de Luce and found her very leaky.

Richard Parsons of St. Botolph, Aldgate, London, draper aged 26. He was purser of the Tristram and Jane which was in Virginia when he saw goods unloaded from the Flower de Luce into a storehouse on Hampton River.

Simon Hake of St. Botolph, Aldgate, London, merchant aged 24. He went as a passenger from London in the Flower de Luce in which he shipped wine, but transferred to the Bonny Bess between Weymouth and Falmouth. Hugh Weston had asserted before a Court in Virginia that the goods on his ship belonged to Joseph Saunders and to his merchant on the ship, William Smith. The Court ordered that nothing was to be sold from the ship until the complaints of her company and passengers had been satisfied. A passenger, John Violett, complained that the steward of the Flower de Luce, Robert Warren, had made free of the passengers' goods on board and had heard the carpenter, William Tayler, say that he had received no wages for his previous 2 voyages. Goods aboard the ship belonged to Arthur Lathberry, ----- Mares, Robert Clarke, Edward Welby, John Stringer, Philip Dodsworth, John Blewett, Edward Searchfield, ----- Lambert and Edward Saunders.

William Stafford of St. Dunstan in the East, London, citizen and grocer of London (gent) aged 36. (2 depositions Vols. 53 & 55). He checked tobacco off the Flower de Luce on behalf of Joseph Saunders and found much of it damaged. The Captains and carpenters employed to view the ship declared she was rotten.

John Bennett of Limehouse, Middlesex, sailor aged 70.

ENGLISH ADVENTURERS

Jonas James of Ratcliffe, Middlesex, sailor aged 59.

Robert Tranchmore of Bermondsey, Surrey, ship carpenter aged 63. He viewed the Flower de Luce and judged that her goods had been damaged by indiscretion and bad stowage.

Robert Warren of Limehouse, Middlesex, sailor aged 29. (2 depositions). He was cooper of the Flower de Luce which sailed from England on 4 August 1636. During the voyage Hugh Weston took sack belonging to William Heywood, a merchant who died on board, and also appropriated other merchants' goods. A merchant, Johnson, who also died on passage, appointed the deponent as overseer of his will.

George Menefie of James City, Virginia, but now resident at St. Helen's, London, merchant aged 40. He has dwelt in Virginia for 16 years. He loaded tobacco in the Flower de Luce for which freight was charged at £5 a ton, and also shipped tobacco in Mr. Fabian's ship. About 20 passengers went home from Virginia in the Flower de Luce and the deponent and 5 of his friends agreed to pay their freight in tobacco. On the return voyage the pumps had to be manned continuously by the ship's company and passengers.

William Greene of St. Katherine, Coleman Street, London, porter aged 37.

Augustine Aldridge of Wapping, Middlesex, ship carpenter aged 41.

John Basill of Limehouse, Middlesex, seaman aged 30. When the Bonny Bess ran ashore at Broken Island off Virginia at Christmas 1636 Hugh Weston took some goods from her which he put ashore in the warehouse of Lieutenant Cheeseman at Nupocosen to await delivery to Mr. Clarke of York, Virginia. After being refloated the Bonny Bess was brought to Kickotan on Weston's orders.

Andrew Reynee of Dunfermline, Scotland, sailor aged

28. He was Master of a ship which he sold in Virginia before shipping himself and his tobacco aboard the Flower de Luce on which he acted as Master's mate. She was an old, rotten ship and left as much tobacco behind in Virginia as she carried home.

Nicholas Strawe of Ratcliffe, Middlesex, mariner aged 31. He was boatswain of the Bonny Bess, Mr. Zachary Flute, which was owned by Smith and Saunders. When she ran aground muskets were fired in order to obtain help from shore. Two boats came out and were loaded but were cast away in the foul weather. The remaining goods in the ship were saved by Weston and delivered to Thomas Burbage.

Matthew Saunders of Whitechapel, Middlesex, yeoman aged 60. He was porter of the London Custom House and saw goods landed from the Flower de Luce.

Leonard Guy of Limehouse, Middlesex, ship carpenter aged 35. He viewed the Flower de Luce and found she was not properly repaired by her owners.

William Tayler of St. Botolph, Aldgate, London, ship carpenter (shipwright) aged 23 (26). (2 depositions). He had made one previous voyage to Virginia in the Merchant Bonadventure, Mr. Harris, before going as carpenter's mate on the Flower de Luce. He succeeded the ship's carpenter when he died. She was freighted to Virginia by Joseph Saunders and William Smith and on her outward voyage Smith and the purser Edward Searchfield as well as many merchants died. Other merchants fell sick and were thus unable to care for their goods which Weston appropriated. The ship leaked so badly on the outward voyage that he had to stop her with beef and after they left Land's End the pumps were manned continuously. (Vols. 53 & 55).

Nicholas Read of Colchester, Essex, sailor aged 31. He shipped strong waters in the Flower de Luce.

John Castle of St. Katherine by the Tower, London, sailor aged 35 (mariner aged 39 in Vol. 55). (2

depositions).   He went as gunner's mate of the <u>Flower
de Luce</u> which shipped 160 passengers for Virginia but
transferred 30 of them at sea into the <u>Bonny Bess</u>.
Hugh Weston threw overboard certain writings of which
some were blown back and found to be Bills of Lading
and invoices which he declared were only waste paper
and good for nothing though he declined to hand them
back to the seaman who retrieved them but said he
would keep them to light his tobacco.   George Menefie
who came home passenger in the <u>Flower de Luce</u> said
he would give his whole estate in her to be ashore with
his child.   (Vols. 53 & 55).

Francis Lathbury, book keeper to Joseph Saunders, aged
24, (of St. Mildred Poultry, London, merchant aged
25/26).   (3 depositions).   Joseph Saunders, to whom he
was apprenticed for 8 years, was the owner of the
<u>Bonny Bess</u> which he bought from John Thierry of
London, merchant, in May or June 1636 for a voyage to
Virginia, and appointed Zachary Flute to go as her
Master.   The deponent paid Thierry his account and
paid the ship's purser, Edward Searchfield, for repairs
carried out on her.   His then master, Joseph Saunders,
received payment from one Clarke for his passage to
Virginia.   After the death of Flute, William Blackler
was elected Master.   The deponent is part owner of the
<u>Truelove</u> which carried passengers from Virginia to
London in 1638 at the rate of £5 or £5.10s. a head.
Those who shipped goods on the <u>Flower de Luce</u>
included his brother Arthur Lathbury of London,
merchant, Edmund Saunders, ----- Penryn, ----- Bradley,
Simon Hake, and Henry Ledgington.   She arrived home
in London before the <u>Bonny Bess</u>.   (Vols. 53 & 54).

Henry Hedly of Limehouse, Middlesex, sailor aged 40.
He has made 2 voyages to Virginia and was chief mate
of the <u>Flower de Luce</u> which shipped 130 or 140
passengers to Virginia at £6 per head.   Jeremy
Loveland brought tobacco home in her.

Thomas Mace of Wapping, Middlesex, sailor aged 48.
He saw Hugh Weston open a trunk belonging to Arthur
Lathbury and knows that he sold goods belonging to

ENGLISH ADVENTURERS

----- Humphreys to Francis Mason in Virginia. William Howard, a passenger to Virginia, died on the voyage.

Thomas Eaton of Wapping, Middlesex, surgeon aged 50. He was surgeon of the <u>Flower de Luce</u>.

John Castle of St. Botolph, Aldgate, London, shipwright aged 24. He was carpenter of the <u>Flower de Luce</u>.

John Browne of Ratcliffe, Middlesex, mariner aged 50. He was a quartermaster of the ship.

William Blackaller of Ratcliffe, Middlesex, mariner aged 35. The <u>Bonny Bess</u> was driven ashore near Long Island before Christmas 1636.

Matthew Longe of Ratcliffe, Middlesex, sailor aged 27. When the <u>Bonny Bess</u> left London her Master was Zachary Flute, her mate William Blackaller, and the boatswain Nicholas Strawe. They and Giles Hallye, one of the ship's company, had goods aboard her. The deponent fell sick on passage and was carried ashore at Virginia.

William Steele of St. Saviour, Southwark, Surrey, weaver aged 34. He was employed to check Hugh Weston's sureties as Master.

William Parsons, servant of William Turner, of All Hallows, Barking, London, cooper, aged 23, deposes re tobacco landed from the <u>Flower de Luce</u>.

Robert Roberts of St. Olave, Southwark, Surrey, silkweaver aged 42, also deposes about the tobacco landed.

Joseph Saunders of London, merchant. His factor in Virginia, Peter Knight, advised him to come to account over the lading of the <u>Flower de Luce</u> with Thomas Burbage.

William Bradshawe of St. Katherine, Coleman Street, London, cooper aged 40. (2 depositions). He shipped as cooper on the Flower de Luce on 1 July 1636 bound for Virginia and returned in her to London. Walter Felton and Roger ----- were hired for the voyage but the latter died on passage. Simon Hake was to have gone passenger to Virginia in her but left her at Weymouth or Falmouth because of the sickness aboard. Most of the wine carried by the ship which belonged to Saunders was drunk by Hugh Weston and others, but what remained was sent into Saunders' warehouse in Virginia. Weston sent home from Virginia tobacco and skins by Mr. Tamage's and Mr. Buckham's ships, and delivered to Mason, a planter in Virginia, a trunk by hand of John Castle, the gunner's mate. (Vols. 53 & 54).

Robert Page of St. Katherine by the Tower, London, sailor aged 32. He has gone as Master of ships on 5 voyages to Virginia and deposes as to wages paid. He knows Henry Hedly, a Master's mate on the Flower de Luce, and he is reputed an honest man. (Vol. 54).

William Barker of Ratcliffe, Middlesex, sailor aged 45. He has made 10 voyages to Virginia as Master or mate. While he was in Virginia in April 1637 he received from the 200 ton Flower de Luce, Mr. Hugh Weston, a supply of bread for which he made reimbursement. Both Thomas Mace and Henry Headley are reputed honest men. (Vol. 54).

Thomas Ashton of Stonedan Hall, Essex, yeoman aged 28. He was put in charge of the goods of William Smith, factor for Joseph Saunders, when he died and was thrown overboard, and of the goods of other merchants when they died, including Mr. William Lathbury and his brother Mr. Arthur Lathbury, and Mr. Werlbye who gave his goods in trust to Philip Dodsworth. But Weston overruled these arrangements and disposed of 6 servants or passengers who belonged to Arthur Lathbury of London, merchant, and also sold cheese to a planter named Perrye at Kikotan in Virginia. (Vol. 54).

William Cropp of Madbury, Devon, sailor aged 48. It

was reputed at Point Comfort, Virginia, while the Bonny Bess was there, that Joseph Saunders had ordered Weston to take charge of her after first having offered her for sale to Leonard Calvert, Governor of Maryland in Virginia. But Saunders had afterwards sold the ship to Richard Orchard. She was then driven on shore by foul weather where she stuck fast and let water so that Orchard was disposed to revoke his bargain until the Governor ordered him to keep to it. The ship was freed with great difficulty, loaded with tobacco, and made the return voyage to London with the deponent as mate. One Davies, pilot of His Majesty's Great Ship, had a son who returned home on the Bonny Bess as did Matthew Longe and the wages of both were paid by Orchard. (Vol. 54).

James Best, servant of Michael Holman of St. Bride's, London, scrivener, aged 20. In May 1636 his then master, Francis Harrison, scrivener, at his shop in the Royal Exchange, received directions from John Thierry, Joseph Saunders or William Smith for a Bill of Sale to be drawn up for the 50 ton ship Bonny Bess. Smith was said to have been a partner with Saunders in a plantation at Virginia. (Vol. 54).

Abraham Giles of Horsey Down, St. Olave, Southwark, Surrey, navigator aged 19. It was generally reported in Virginia that Hugh Weston had sold the Bonny Bess to Richard Orchard and the deponent rowed both men aboard her from Weston's ship, the Flower de Luce, at Point Comfort. When the Bonny Bess ran ashore Weston's men belonging to the America helped to retrieve her. The America sailed from Virginia to London in December 1637 and arrived in June 1638. (Vol. 54).

William Kinge of Redriffe, Surrey, sailor aged 29. He was boatswain of the America which returned to London in company with the Bonny Bess which was forced by contrary winds to put into the Isle of Wight where Orchard put beer aboard. (Vol. 54).

Abraham Orten of St. Sepulchre, London, mariner aged

60. He was employed to go as cook in the Flower de Luce to Virginia and she went in company with the Bonny Bess, both having been set out by Joseph Saunders. Some of the goods salvaged from the latter ship were brought ashore on Captain Thurrygood's plantation. (Vol. 54).

William Sherman of All Hallows, Barking, London, cooper aged 27. In August 1636, when he was a servant to Thomas Norden of London, wine cooper, he delivered wine aboard the Flower de Luce on behalf of Simon Hacke to be delivered to Virginia. (Vol. 54).

John White of St. Sepulchre, London, grocer aged 35. The tobacco brought to London in the Flower de Luce proved mostly rotten and Francis Lathbury bought part of it. Stafford, Joseph Saunders' agent, kept the key of the warehouse where the tobacco was stored. (Vol. 54).

Thomas Leddoze of Weymouth, Dorset, merchant aged 51. He was part owner of the Flower de Luce which he freighted to Saunders. The tobacco she brought back from Virginia was damaged by water and the deponent and others have brought suit in this court. (Vol. 54).

Samuel Peirce of St. Mary Abchurch, London, merchant aged 24. On 11 October 1638 the Flower de Luce, Mr. John White, sailed from Newfoundland to Virginia where she arrived at Point Comfort on 21 October and at James City on 2 November 1638. The ship's freighters, George Grace, Nicholas Scourfield and Simon Hake went with the deponent as passengers. On 11 April 1639 the ship left Point Comfort for home. John White and the ship's purser, Samuel Leddoze, had told her freighters that they were prepared to take additional freight on board. When she arrived back at Weymouth, Grace and Hake left her to travel overland to London and the deponent left her at Dover. (Vol. 54).

Morgan Guilliams of Weymouth, Dorset, sailor aged 45. The freighters had complained to him in Virginia about the lack of lading for the ship's homeward voyage. (Vol. 54).

Thomas Davis of Chuckatucke, Virginia, merchant aged 26. He was a witness to the protest entered by White and Leddoze in Virginia against the freighters for insufficient lading. The deponent put goods aboard the Flower de Luce to be shipped to London. At Dover she was met by some of the King's ships and ordered to proceed to London for which her Master was required to give his bond of £1000. (Vol. 54).

George Pitt of Weymouth, sailor aged 44, deposes as above. (Vol. 54).

Henry Walton of All Hallows, Barking, London, grocer aged 24. He was appointed to appraise the value of the tobacco which was well decayed. (Vol. 54).

John Williams of Crutched Friars, London, merchant aged 46, deposes as to the causes of decay in tobacco. (Vol. 54).

Michael Meysey of St. Katherine, Coleman Street, London, gent aged 37. He was a Messenger of the London Custom House and viewed the lading of the Flower de Luce when she arrived in London in 1637. (Vol. 55).

Hugh Crosse of Weymouth, Dorset, sailor aged 46. The Flower de Luce carried at least 140 passengers for Virginia. When Mr. William Smith and other merchants on board died, Hugh Weston went to the hold, opened their trunks, and took their goods into his cabin. These merchants' executors complained to the Governor when they arrived in Virginia about Weston's conduct. (Vol. 55).

Richard Ingle of Bermondsey, Surrey, sailor aged 30. When the Flower de Luce arrived in Virginia in November 1637, Nicholas Clarke and Mr. Stevenson, planters resident there, brought a suit before the Quarter Court against Hugh Weston for embezzlement of the goods of Mr. Humfries, a passenger on the ship who had died. Peter Knight, Joseph Saunders' factor in Virginia, made satisfaction in tobacco which was shipped aboard the Flower de Luce for London. (Vol. 55).

David Hutton of Shadwell, Middlesex, sailor aged 31. The suit in Virginia against Knight and Burbage was begun in December 1637. (Vol. 55).

THE KING & ----- BETTANY v. HENRY TAVERNER. 1 August 1637 to 22 February 1637/8.

Nicholas Harrison of St. Katherine by the Tower, London, but born at Canterbury, Kent, surgeon aged 38 (42). (2 depositions). Richard Field, a passenger to Virginia in the Elizabeth and Sarah, of which Mr. Henry Taverner was Master and Edmond Turner chief mate, fell sick of the dropsy and at his own request was put ashore when the ship had to put into Falmouth because of bad weather. The deponent advised Field to make a will leaving part of his estate to his sworn brother, the ship's boatswain Thomas Smith, but instead he left his whole estate to Edmond Turner who, in turn, wished Taverner to have his whole estate. Turner began to make a note of Field's goods on board but, being called to prayer, said he would complete the list later. During the outward voyage Turner wagered a passenger Mary Deane some clothing that she would be unable to keep watch for 3 days and nights without sleeping but she lost by falling asleep within 6 hours. Nevertheless she retained the clothing after her master, a merchant named Holmes, had paid for it. Edmond Turner died before the ship reached Virginia and all his and Richard Field's goods were sold there. On the return voyage to London they encountered a wreck off the English coast which Taverner fastened for 23 hours during which time he removed from it oil, silk and money.

John Smith of Redriffe, Surrey, but born at Burntisland, Scotland, sailor aged 30. When the Elizabeth and Sarah encountered the floating wreckage on her return voyage, Taverner threatened with his pistol those of his ship's company who wanted to prise open the chests which were salvaged.

Marmaduke Crosby of Wapping, Middlesex, pilot aged 23. Turner was born at Homas, Spalden Moor, Yorkshire. When he made his wager with Mary Deane he was in a drunken fit.

ROBERT WHITMORE v. JOSEPH BLOWE & ABRAHAM HOPKINSON. 10 October to 6 November 1637.

Joseph Jordan, servant of John Southwood of St. Martin, Ironmonger Lane, merchant, aged 24. In June 1637 he paid Abraham Hopkinson, part owner of the Tristram and Jane, Mr. Joseph Blowe, for tobacco shipped from Virginia on account of Robert Whitmore and for the passage home of Mrs. Whitmore. The tobacco was not delivered.

William Bateman of St. Martin, Ironmonger Lane, London, merchant aged 25. Robert Whitmore has a plantation and servants in Virginia and, had he received his tobacco from the Tristram and Jane, would have returned with other planters to Virginia in May or June. He was unable to leave until August.

William Melyn of St. Stephen, Coleman Street, London, merchant aged 60. He had weighed tobacco to be delivered to John Southwood, assignee of Whitmore.

John Dansey of All Hallows, Barking, London, gent aged 46, deposes as to the value of tobacco brought from Virginia.

John Glascocke of St. Olave, Hart Street, London, gent aged 45, deposes similarly.

John Digby of St. Andrew Hubbard, London, citizen and pewterer of London aged 45.

William Godfrey of All Hallows, Barking, London,

citizen and cordwainer of London aged 36.

Edward Pitt of All Hallows, Barking, London, yeoman aged 49. He saw Whitmore's tobacco delivered to a warehouse in London.

Francis Harris of St. Katherine by the Tower, London, sailor aged 29. While the Tristram and Jane was at Virginia she was strong but after she met bad weather on her return voyage she became leaky. She arrived in London on 5 or 6 April 1637.

JOHN CUTTINGE v. JAMES BROCKE.   20 October 1637.

Henry Lever of Ipswich, Suffolk, ship carpenter aged 43. He knew James Brocke in New England where he had gone as a Master's mate in a ship from London, returning to England as a passenger in the New Supply of which John Cuttinge was Master and part owner. Brocke, a fat, heavy man, was very abusive to Cuttinge, calling his vessel "a ship of rushes" and questioning his skill as a mariner, for which Cuttinge struck him.

Robert Price of Ipswich, Suffolk, sailor aged 27.

RICHARD BRADSHAW v. THE SPEELE YACHT.   20 November 1637.

Thomas Gilmett of St. Sepulchre, London, haberdasher aged 37. He booked a passage for himself and his goods to New England in the 100 ton Elizabeth of London of which the owners were Richard Bradshawe, Eustace Man & Co. When she was bilged by the action of the Dutchmen at Pendennis Castle her owners lost £3000 or £4000.

(See also **RE THE ELIZABETH,** p. 36).

FOR JOSHUA MULLARD AND ELIZABETH HIS WIFE, WIDOW OF WILLIAM HOLMES GENT DECEASED. 29 January 1637/8.

Captain Samuel Mathew of Denby, Virginia. In 1624 he received from Captain William Holmes in Virginia a note of the tobaccos due to him and to Abraham Peirce. The bills included tobaccos due from William Muche, Thomas Bunn, Captain William Peirce, Captain Roger Smith, Christopher Hall, John Carter, William Spencer, Richard Peirce, ----- Osborne, Francis Wyatt, Anthony Barum, Thomas Parsemore, Captain Wilcocks, Walter Scott and Thomas Salvage. The deponent owed Holmes for a house he had bought from him which was his brother's Rouslie's. When Douglas Marriner arrived in Virginia from London he brought news that Holmes had been killed outward bound for Virginia whereupon the deponent delivered his bills to Abraham Peirce, a merchant living in Virginia but since deceased. Those bills he held from Wilcocks, Scott and Salvage he delivered to Charles Harmer. Scott died worth nothing but the deponent had provided for his widow. When Abraham Peirce settled his debt of tobacco to Holmes it was placed in a warehouse at James Town in 1627 but by Christmas that year no one had claimed it and by that time the deponent had sold his plantation. When he sent for the tobacco to be brought to his new plantation his servants accidentally set fire to it. At the beginning of 1628 Captain Hedland was told of this mishap when he demanded the tobacco from the deponent. In the same year the deponent gave a bill to Captain Holmes' widow for payment of the tobacco he owed.

VOLUME 54

RE THE ELIZABETH OF LONDON. 4 June 1638 to 20 February 1638/9.

John Lillie of York, Virginia, planter aged 30, for Mr. Joseph Hawes. On 10 October 1637 the Elizabeth of London, Mr. Benjamin Woolmer, was on course for

Virginia when she was surprised and captured off Bermuda by Spanish galleons and taken to Cadiz. The deponent had freighted goods in the Elizabeth on his own behalf and in trust for Mistress Ulye for which he will be accountable when he arrives in Virginia to which he is now bound.

Oliver Downe of Cheesecake, Virginia, planter aged 46. In July 1637 he loaded on the Elizabeth goods and 3 servants who were bound to him for 7 years. He has received no profit from his plantation and servants in Virginia because of the taking of the ship.

Peter Talbott of St. Dunstan in the West, London, gent aged 43. His estimated loss on goods he loaded in the Elizabeth is £20.

Richard Perrin of All Hallows, Barking, London, late planter in Virginia, aged 26. He has land in Virginia which he intended to stock and plant from goods carried in the Elizabeth and estimates his loss at £40.

Stephen Webb of James City, Virginia, planter aged 39. He and his wife and children went as passengers on the Elizabeth and were taken to Cadiz. There he was kept prisoner and forced to work as a slave for 8 months. He lost his goods and 3 servants who were captured with him for whose passage he had paid £6 a head. He estimates his loss at £450.

Thomas Browne of Kingsman Neck, Virginia, planter aged 33. He paid for the passage of himself, his wife and for goods on the Elizabeth and estimates his loss at £100.

William Bell of Chigwell, Essex, yeoman aged 21. In mid July 1637 he loaded goods for Virginia on the Elizabeth.

John Kersey of Dublin, Ireland, merchant aged 35. He lost goods aboard the Elizabeth which was taken by the King of Spain's ships in December 1637.

ENGLISH ADVENTURERS

William Willoughby of Wapping, Middlesex, shipwright aged 52. He owned a quarter share of the <u>Elizabeth</u>.

John Higgins of Wapping, Middlesex, mariner aged 58. He was gunner of the <u>Elizabeth</u> whose Bills of Lading were delivered in Madrid by the Master's mate.

Benjamin Woolmer of Ratcliffe, Middlesex, mariner aged 46. He was Master of the 150 ton <u>Elizabeth</u> which carried 10 guns and left London on 20 July 1637 for a trading voyage to Virginia. On 11 October she was intercepted 250 leagues from Virginia by 11 Spanish ships, part of the Plate Fleet, and her whole company excepting only some women and servants were taken aboard the Spanish Admiral's ship. The Admiral contended that the King of Spain had jurisdiction in those parts and that the King of England had no rights there. The Bills of Lading were taken to the British Ambassador in Spain.

John Cooke of Ipswich, Suffolk, mariner aged 30. He was a quartermaster of the <u>Elizabeth</u>.

Richard Manning of St. Katherine by the Tower, London, mariner aged 32. He was boatswain.

(see also **MANWARING v. DESSAREY, p. 112.**)

WILLIAM DOUGLAS v. FRANCIS SMITH. 18 June 1638.

Thomas Nevison, servant of William Douglas, aged 18. His master employed Francis Smith as his factor to recover debts in Virginia and in August 1636 the deponent accompanied him to Virginia where Smith received tobacco on his master's account from John Brush, planter, Mr. John Neale, merchant then residing in Virginia, Alexander Gardiner, planter, John Haynie, planter, and Captain Henry Browne. In June 1637 Francis Smith and the deponent returned from Virginia together with tobacco for which Smith refused to come to account, being now bound out on another voyage to Virginia.

STEPHEN GORTON & FRANCIS FOWLER v. ISAAC WATLINGTON. GILES WILFORD v. RICHARD PARSONS. 23 March 1637/8 to 20 November 1639.

Robert Redhead of Rochester, Kent, mariner aged 30. He was boatswain's mate of HMS Swiftsure which in March 1637/8 intercepted the Truelove of London, Mr. Isaac Watlington, which was loaded with Virginia tobacco, and ordered her to London. While the Truelove was off Margate Francis Lathbury came out to her in a boat and returned with Watlington to the town after which the ship sailed for Holland on 16 March 1637/8. (Vol. 53).

Thomas White of St. Sepulchre, London, merchant aged 24. (2 depositions). In March 1637/8 when the Truelove was off Dover the wind was set fair for London. In May 1638 when he was resident in Rotterdam the Truelove arrived there with tobacco and the deponent went aboard as the assignee of Stephen Gorton to seek delivery of his tobacco from Isaac Watlington and the purser, Richard Parsons, but they refused even when Joseph Saunders came to Rotterdam to claim it. While the ship was in Rotterdam she took aboard tobacco from Francis Fowler to be delivered to John White of London, grocer.

William Clarke of Shoe Lane, London, distiller aged 29. In February 1637/8 Stephen Gorton came from Virginia in the Truelove with tobacco which he sold to John White of London, grocer. When Gorton was in danger of death in November 1638 the deponent and John White went to see him and Gorton then confirmed that he had made the sale.

Margaret Waters, wife of John Waters of Ratcliffe, Middlesex, sailor, aged 35. Giles Wilford went as a common sailor in the Truelove to Virginia in Spring 1638. On her return Margaret Wilford, then in childbed, asked the deponent to go to Richard Parsons, her purser, to enquire after her husband. The deponent went to Parsons' house in St. Katherine's and was told that Giles Wilford had died but was promised £1.

ENGLISH ADVENTURERS

Christopher Barwicke. The <u>Truelove</u> returned from Holland to London at Easter 1638 when he went with Margaret Wilford to the Three Cranes Tavern in the Poultry, where the ship's company were to receive their wages, to collect the money raised by the sale of Wilford's clothing. Margaret Wilford was then told that she could not be paid until Richard Parsons returned from Holland.

Katherine Silver, wife of John Silver of Ratcliffe, Middlesex, sailor, aged 30. Richard Parsons was arrested in September 1638 at the suit of Margaret Wilford and he confessed that he had sold tobacco belonging to Giles Wilford.

Richard Cooper of Stepney, Middlesex, anchorsmith aged 40. Richard Parsons confessed to him that he had sold tobacco belonging to Giles Wilford.

Francis Bristowe of ?Ware, Herts, merchant aged 37. When the <u>Truelove</u> arrived in Rotterdam in March 1637/8 laden with Virginia tobacco Thomas White, factor for Francis Fowler, demanded 8 hogsheads from Watlington but was refused.

Francis Bristowe of St. Margaret, New Fish Street, waterman (acquarius) aged 37, deposes as above. (Vol. 55).

Thomas Ashbye of St. Botolph, Aldgate, London, sailor aged 40. He has lived by the sea for 30 years and went as gunner of the <u>Truelove</u> on which Giles Wilford shipped as trumpeter. Wilford died on the return voyage from Virginia having put his tobacco in the charge of the purser who took and sold it. (Vol. 55).

Gilbert Hutton of Shadwell, Middlesex, sailor aged 22. When he returned from Virginia in 1638 Wilford asked Richard Parsons to make out his will and to take care of his estate for the benefit of his widow and children. (Vol. 55).

Robert Millner of Wapping, Middlesex, sailor aged 23.

He has been to sea for 8 years and shared Wilford's mess on the Truelove. (Vol. 55).

James White of Ratcliffe, Middlesex, sailor aged 35. He has lived by the sea for 20 years and served on the Truelove to Virginia and Rotterdam. (Vol. 55).

John White of St. Sepulchre, London, grocer aged 35. Francis Fowler wrote to him from Virginia to inform him that tobacco had been loaded aboard the Truelove to his account to be brought to London. (Vol. 55).

Thomas Celye of All Hallows, Barking, London, merchant aged 43. In January 1637/8 tobacco was loaded on the Truelove to be taken to London on Gorton's account. (Vol. 55).

Richard Ingle of St. Mary Magdalene, Bermondsey, Surrey, sailor aged 30. He was Master's mate of the Truelove which arrived off the Downs in March 1637/8 when the wind was set fair for London but she proceeded to Rotterdam where she unloaded tobacco. Within a week of her arrival there it was reported that 2 other ships loaded with tobacco had arrived at Flushing and advice was received from London that still more tobacco ships were due in Holland. This had the effect of depressing tobacco prices there. On his return to London on 20 March 1637/8 he found a proclamation had been posted forbidding the landing of tobacco anywhere in the Kingdom except London. He approached Gorton to ask him to end his suit in favour of an out-of-court settlement. (Vol. 55).

Joseph Saunders of St. Mildred Poultry, London, merchant aged 39. When the Truelove arrived off the Downs the wind was fair for Holland so she went there instead of to London for which the wind was contrary. He and Mr. Fuller freighted the ship and his brother John White and Francis Bristowe were in partnership for the tobacco she carried. (Vol. 55).

Francis Lathbury of St. Mildred Poultry, London, aged 27. He had read the proclamation about the landing of tobaccos in London. He had in his hands £700 belonging to Watlington of which £400 had been attached on behalf of Gorton but the latter had refused to come to account. (Vol. 55).

Jeremiah Loveland of St. Ma-----, London, merchant aged 34, deposes re tobacco prices. The proclamation about landing of tobaccos was made on 15 March 1637/8. (Vol. 55).

David Nicholson of Disert, Scotland, sailor aged 28. He was boatswain of the Truelove and knows that Giles Wilford's tobacco was sold at Rotterdam. (Vol. 56).

William Jeanes of St. Botolph, Aldgate, London, cooper aged 25. He saw Wilford buy tobacco from the inhabitants of Virginia. (Vol. 56).

WILLIAM CROSSE v. JAMES AUSTREY. WILLIAM PECKETT v. FRANCIS SMITH & WILLIAM HILL. 13 October 1638 to 9 May 1639.

John Ivatt of Limehouse, Middlesex, sailor aged 30. He was boatswain of the Elizabeth, Mr. John Fareborne, on which William Hill served as Master's mate and Francis Smith as ship's merchant and factor. On a voyage to Virginia Fareborne died off Bermuda having asked Smith to assume command after him. But Hill threatened to leave the ship if this happened and then became Master with Smith's consent. Some of Fareborne's goods were sold at the mast while others were taken by Hill and sold by him in Virginia for tobacco.

John Backenhurst, servant of William Crosse, aged 22. John Fairborne was Master and part owner of the Elizabeth and went with Francis Smith in September 1637 to the house of William Crosse in Botolph Lane, London, with a bill of bottomry for the ship which was then intended for Virginia.

John Mainett of St. Bartholomew by the Exchange, London, notary public aged 39, deposes as above.

ENGLISH ADVENTURERS

George Barker, servant of Jone de Peister, of St. George, Botolph Lane, London, merchant aged 24. He has seen the charter party for the <u>Elizabeth</u>'s voyage to Virginia. Because the owners could not set up their ship for the voyage they were forced to take money on bottomry and the deponent witnessed their bond. The ship returned to London with Virginia tobacco in April or May 1638.

Martin Dallison of St. Christopher le Stocks, London, scrivener aged 31. He made out the charter party for the ship of which Morrice Thompson and other owners were the freighters. On 18 September 1637 Fairborne borrowed money from James Austrey to set up his ship for the voyage.

Richard Cole of Stepney, Middlesex, sailor aged 33. He went as carpenter of the <u>Elizabeth</u> to Virginia in Michaelmas 1637. When she was 7 or 8 weeks into the voyage John Fareborne died and William Hill assumed command. Some of Fareborne's goods were sold on board and others delivered to William Warren in Virginia who came aboard and declared that he was answerable for all Fareborne's goods delivered to his house. His servants John Hampton and Walter Price had confessed that they owed Warren for tobacco.

Thomas Beckett of Stepney, Middlesex, aged 25. He went as cooper of the <u>Elizabeth</u> of which Francis Smith was purser and merchant for Mr. Willoughby and Mr. Thompson.

Joseph Medlye of Battersea, Surrey, waterman aged 30. He delivered goods on board the <u>Elizabeth</u> while she lay at Gravesend. His brother John Medlye who lived at the Three Cranes Tavern at the Vintry, London, also adventured goods on the voyage. (Vol. 55).

JOHN LOVELAND v. OLIVER NEAVE. 10 November 1638.

John Brokenden of the City of London, merchant aged

47.   In October 1632 he, John Loveland and William Giles freighted the <u>Bonadventure</u>, Mr. Richard Bonner, to carry lead and red herrings to Naples (<u>etc. etc.</u>). Thomas Kerridge was joint adventurer with the deponent and Oliver Neave joint adventurer with Loveland.   John Loveland died indebted to the deponent and was to have repaid him with tobacco to be delivered in Virginia.

----- **GLANVILL v.** ----- **BRIGGS.**   20 November 1638.

Gilbert Grimes of Ratcliffe, Middlesex, sailor aged 33, deposes as to wages paid to ships' Masters.   He has sailed from London to the West Indies for 8 years and has made 3 voyages as a Master but was never at Virginia.

Benjamin Bowden of Ratcliffe, Middlesex, sailor aged 36.   He has made several voyages to Virginia, twice as a Master, and on one of these as Master of the <u>Elizabeth</u>.

THOMAS COLE v. MATTHEW SMITH.   18 February 1638/9.

William Colton of St. Mary at Hill, London, waterman aged 26.   A year ago Thomas Cole sold clothing to Matthew Smith for which payment was to be made in Virginia tobacco.   The deponent, Cole and Smith arrived in London from Virginia at Easter 1638.

----- **BOWDEN v.** ----- **PEASELYE.** (<u>Dispute re wages</u>). 13 February 1638/9.

Henry Fabian of Limehouse, Middlesex, sailor aged 39. He has been a Master of ships for 20 years and has made several voyages to Virginia.

Christopher Moulthropp of Ratcliffe, Middlesex, sailor aged 26.   He has been a ship's Master on 2 voyages to Barbados.

ENGLISH ADVENTURERS

VOLUME 55

CHRISTOPHER MALYN v. MAURICE THOMPSON.
4 to 28 October 1639.

Thomas Silver of Redriffe, Surrey, sailor aged 34. He went to Virginia in 1635 as carpenter of the Paul, Mr. Leonard Betts, and when he went ashore there he made the acquaintance of Edward Bateman and saw there an old wooden ship, much worm eaten and unfit to go to sea, called the Elizabeth. Maurice Thompson freighted the Paul and consigned her lading to his factor in Virginia, Mr. (Thomas) Stagge. The merchant of the ship was Mr. Middleton. While she was at Virginia Edward Bateman, who was a ship's carpenter, was employed for 10 weeks in making repairs and expressed a desire to return to England as carpenter of the America whose own carpenter had died, but Stagge claimed that he had purchased Bateman's indentures of service from his master Christopher Malyn, and Bateman himself confessed that he had received a suit of clothes in part payment of his wages. Stagge warned the deponent that Bateman was likely to forsake his work, hide, and then hire himself to the America before the Paul left Virginia. Stagge was known in Virginia as a great and well beloved man.

Leonard Betts of Wapping, Middlesex, sailor aged 36. While he was in Virginia he heard that Maurice Thomnpson had paid Christopher Malyn for the time spent by Bateman in making repairs to the Paul.

JOHN JOHNS v. PERCIVAL POTTS. 18 & 19 October 1639.

James Bucklye of Shadwell, Middlesex, sailor aged 33. He was of the company of the Blessing, Mr. Hill, which was freighted to Virginia by John Johns. She left Gravesend on 12 October 1638 but, being without wind at the Downs for 3 weeks, put into the Isle of Wight where her leaks were stopped and Captain Holson taken on board as a passenger. She remained there for 2 months and after a 7 weeks' voyage arrived in Virginia on Ash Wednesday 1639. When he went ashore at Kikatan the deponent heard Robert Johns and Percival Potts discussing her lading for the return voyage and the Master said he was willing to take all the tobacco which Potts wished to load but was not prepared to receive tobacco from a Plymouth ship which had been cast away in Virginia. After a 5 week stay in Virginia the Blessing sailed for home.

Edward Budden of St. Augustine, London, embroiderer aged 33. He went as purser of the Blessing and while she was in Virginia boats were sent to Potts' plantation to collect tobacco but Potts turned them away, preferring to send his tobacco to Mr. Minifie's ship.

MARY LIMBRIE v. ----- WILLSON. 8 January 1639/40.

Richard Cooper of Ratcliffe, Middlesex, but born at Worwall, Cheshire, sailor aged 73. While he was in Amsterdam he received from Lawrence Coughen an account of tobaccos shipped from St. Christopher's to the account of Mary Limbrie. Coughen had received from Mary Limbrie a letter of attorney authorising him to demand tobaccos of Willson for herself or her husband which he (Willson) had acquired in Virginia while attending to Mary Limbrie's business there.

----- BRADLEY & THOMAS STAGGE v. JOHN ROSE, ----- MARTYN & ----- BUDD. 11 January 1639/40 & 26 June 1641.

Robert Barker of Great Yarmouth, sailor aged 22. He was boatswain of the Susanna as apprentice to one of her owners, William Buttolphe. While she was at Virginia in June 1639 Thomas Stagge loaded a bale of beaver to be delivered to London but when the ship arrived home many of the outer skins had been eaten by rats. The bale was put on a lighter in the Thames said to belong to Mr. Lucey.

Thomas Covell of Whitechapel, Middlesex, gent aged 52. He was a waiter at the London Custom House in 1639 and surveyed the goods brought in by the Susanna, Mr. John Rose, from Virginia. They included a bale of beaver skins small enough to be carried under a man's arm. (Vol. 57).

GEORGE MINIFIE v. ----- COCKETT, ----- SMITH & ----- MASON. EDWARD WOOD & RICHARD BATSON v. ----- CHAMBERLAINE. 17 February 1639/40 to 3 October 1640.

Robert Gurling of Ipswich, Suffolk, sailor aged 41. He was Master of the Dove which was freighted by Wood, Batson and Minifie for a voyage to Virginia. After she put into Cowes, Isle of Wight, to take Minifie's goods on board she was detained by contrary winds for a month and during that time the 106 passengers embarked for Virginia seriously depleted the provisions. She was therefore obliged to put into Plymouth to restock and stayed there 3 days. Because she then met cross winds she was obliged to put into Falmouth. After she arrived at Virginia a Mr. Saunderson sent tobacco aboard and despatched some of the ship's company to collect more but none was forthcoming from any of the places they visited. The Dove stayed at Virginia for over a month and took back over 50 tons of freight to London.

John Leech of Ipswich, Suffolk, sailor aged 21. He served on the Dove which loaded goods at James Town, Virginia.

John Burchett of St. Dunstan in the East, London, grocer (servant of Edward Wood) aged 26. (2 depositions). He was a witness to the charter party by which Wood and Batson freighted the Dove from Gurling. She arrived back in London in August 1639 with tobacco marked for Mr. Chamberlaine. (Vol. 56).

Patrick Strelley of All Hallows, Barking, London, gent aged 38, deposes similarly. (Vol. 56).

ENGLISH ADVENTURERS

Grace Hardwyn of St. Michael, Crooked Lane, London, wax chandler aged 45. He was part owner of the William of London, Mr. Anthony Austen, which landed Virginia tobacco in London in July 1638 marked for Mr. Chamberlaine. (Vol. 56).

George Faulkener of York, Virginia, merchant aged 24. George Minifie came from Virginia in the Dove in 1638 and delivered to a warehouse in Bear Lane, London, tobacco marked for Mr. Chamberlaine to whom the deponent was then a servant. (Vol. 56).

WILLIAM CLEBORNE v. ----- CLOBERY. ----- SMITH, & ----- FRANCKLYN v. ----- MOREHEAD & ----- CLOBERY.
5 March 1639/40 to 10 November 1642.

Thomas Grinder of St. Saviour, Southwark, Surrey, victualler aged 43. He was William Cleborne's servant when the Africa arrived at the Isle of Kent, Virginia and unloaded goods into warehouses there. 10 or 12 days afterwards there occurred a disastrous fire which destroyed both the warehouses and their contents. Cleborne immediately wrote to Clobery & Co. and to Mr. James, Minister of that plantation, to ask for further supplies to be sent there urgently in order to maintain the Isle of Kent settlement but for over 3 years nothing was received. At last a small consignment came by the Mayflower, Mr. Andrewes. The deponent who was closely acquainted with Cleborne, having supped with him almost every day for 8 years, knew how much he had lost from his personal fortune because of these events. The plantation was left in great misery and want and in danger of destruction by the Indians because the fire had destroyed their munitions. Cleborne himself, however, was so beloved of the Indians that he could achieve more in trade with them for beaver skins than any other man although it was always necessary in that trade to send out parties of not less than 7 men for their protection. Cleborne had once been captured by the Indians and would undoubtedly have been killed had he not been rescued. Moreover, because of the hardship inflicted upon the plantation Cleborne had lost the use of his right arm by being obliged to sleep on the ground or on boards or in the woods.

After the fire Cleborne sent into the surrounding country for corn and brought in his own 50 head of cattle in order to provide milk and food for the plantation. It is usual in Virginia for a planter or freeman to give 100 weight of tobacco for a year's use of a milch cow and, at the end of that time, to return the cow to her owner with her increase. With his own money Cleborne hired 10 servants from the surrounding parts to come and tend the plantation. At his first arrival there he had found most of the servants on the Isle of Kent plantation sick and unable to provide food for themselves, in no condition to resist any Indian attack. Many of the chief men who came over in the Africa died and many who survived were also sick. Two men who died at the plantation were John Belson and Henry Ubancke.

The goods which came in the Africa were intended to be traded for corn to be shipped to New England and Nova Scotia and part to be used to buy hogs for the plantation.

Robert Turtle of St. Giles, Cripplegate, London, carpenter aged 54. He was aboard the pinnace John Goodfellow in Kecotan harbour and ferried servants to the Sarah and Elizabeth to be shipped by Clobery and Morehead on behalf of George Evelyn to the Isle of Kent which was 50 leagues distant. When he was preparing to leave for England Cleborne offered to Evelyn all his possessions in the Isle of Kent but Evelyn refused. Mr. John Butler had no part in the dealings between the two. When Evelyn took possession of the Isle of Kent he appointed servants Howell Morgan, Thomas White, John Sturman, Roger Baxter and Mathew Royden to make pipe staves. They worked with Thomas Sturman and Thomas ?Kevecorops to make 50,000 staves before the Governor of Maryland took possession of them. The deponent was appointed by Evelyn to be the millwright, to grind corn at the mill and to make cogwheels for it.   William Porter was appointed to act in his stead when the deponent was absent. Evelyn freed Original ?Brawne, sold Thomas Audley, sold the remaining time of John Scarborough to Serjeant Haywarde, sold to John Walker his remaining time, and sold Vincent Mansfield's remaining time to Nicholas Wright.   He placed Mountjoy Evelyn at Potomack River to learn the country's language. Without authority he transported to Maryland for his own gain John Ayscough, Edward Deering, Andrew Baker and Thomas Baker his son, William Williamson and his wife, John Hatch, Philip West, John Dandy and John Hobson.

After Cleborne's departure from the plantation Evelyn went 3 or 4 times to Maryland where he obtained a Commission under the Maryland seal proclaiming him commander of the Isle of Kent.

Maurice Thompson of St. Andrew Hubbard, London, merchant aged 36.   He met Cleborne and Clobery several times in 1630 and 1631 to discuss the settlement of a plantation at the Isle of Kent where a joint stock adventure was planned to be managed by Cleborne who was to go in the Africa while Clobery, who expected a great profit from the venture, was to obtain a patent for free trade there.   After his arrival at the Isle of Kent Cleborne wrote to Clobery advising him of a fire there which had burned many of the beaver skins.   In the following summer the London partners sent out further supplies though less than the full amount Cleborne had asked for.   The deponent gave Clobery, now deceased, a full account of how he had equipped the Africa at Gravesend and Deal when she was outward bound and at that time Cleborne told him that he had, or would obtain, cattle in Virginia which he would transport to the Isle of Kent.   (Vol. 56).

Samuel Smith of St. Sepulchre by Newgate, London, gent aged 22.   He was in Virginia with Cleborne who deserved a good recompense for his employment there.

He saw cattle belonging to Sir Thomas Gates loaded into 3 pinnaces at Kekotan to be transported to the Isle of Kent. That plantation suffered great want of powder and ammunition and was in danger of being deserted because of the threat from the Indians. Cleborne's care and industry was undone by the Marylanders who surprised and captured the boats and pinnaces and killed some men. For want of a Patent Cleborne suffered great loss. Trading with the Indians is very dangerous because of their treachery and thievery and it is always necessary to send 6 or 7 men in a shallop or pinnace for the purpose, sometimes guarded by 200 or 300 men. The Indians are so cunning that they steal even with their toes. Evelyn had spoken against the pretended right of the Marylanders (to possession of the Isle of Kent) and ill of the Governor of Maryland, but some of the inhabitants of the Isle of Kent said the Governor had not molested the island because Evelyn carried a Commission from him. (Vol. 57).

Richard Orchard of Wapping, Middlesex, sailor aged 40. He has lived in Maryland and Virginia for 2 years and has often seen the Patent granted to Lord Baltimore for the Province of Maryland. The Isle of Kent or Isle of Contentment of Virginia is north of the 40 degree line and the greater part is therefore outside the bounds of Maryland. (Vol. 57).

Thomas Stagge of St. Catherine Creechurch, London, merchant aged 39. When he was at the Isle of Kent in May 1639 Leonard Calvert offered to sell him 50,000 pipe staves. He was afterwards in Maryland with Calvert and Lewgar, secretaries to Lord Baltimore, and heard them discussing the ownership of the staves. (Vol. 57).

Richard Ingle of St. Mary Magdalene, Bermondsey, Surrey, sailor aged 33. He was Master of the Richard and Anne and while he was at the port of St. Mary's in Maryland agreed with the then Governor, Leonard Calvert, to take 40,000 pipe staves from the Isle of Kent to London. He was at the Isle of Kent in March

1640/41 and has since heard that Lord Baltimore had seized the island. (Vol. 58).

Robert Turtle of St. Giles, Cripplegate, London, carpenter aged 60. (2nd deposition). He was at the Isle of Kent plantation in 1636 when it was planted and inhabited. A fort was built there for its defence under the Government of Virginia. Cleborne was appointed Governor and built houses, a windmill and a smith's forge and the inhabitants were in reasonable and quiet possession for 5 or 6 years. In 1636 or 1637 Leonard Calvert and Captain Cornwallis came to the island to claim it for Maryland and those of the inhabitants who resisted were imprisoned and 2 were executed. At that time 60,000 or 70,000 weight of tobacco was growing there and there were 60 or 70 servants young and old of all sorts, 200 head of cattle, and 40,000 or 50,000 pipe staves. (Vol. 58).

VOLUME 56

JOHN ONIONS v. THE HOPE. 17 June 1640.

John Onions of Plymouth, Devon, shipwright aged 47. In 1635 he shipped as carpenter on the Hope of Ipswich, Mr. Gurling, for a voyage to New England after which she was intended for the Isle of May. But contrary winds forced her to Barbados where she took a lading of cotton and tobacco before returning to London.

(see also **VENNARD v. VANE**, p. 67ff).

FOR COLE. 2 July 1640.

Edward Godney of St. Andrew Hubbard, London, grocer aged 25. On 24 April 1640 he viewed 26 hogsheads of Virginia tobacco brought to London by the George and found the greatest part decayed.

SIMON TURGESS v. JOSEPH SAUNDERS.
6 July to 11 November 1640.

Matthew Longe of Ratcliffe, Middlesex, sailor aged 32. He went to Virginia in the Bonny Bess to accompany the Admiral ship Flower de Luce, Mr. Hugh Weston, both ships in the employ of Joseph Saunders. At Virginia Weston sold the Bonny Bess to Mr. Orchard by agreement with the Governor of Virginia and, after she had been driven on shore, the deponent helped to retrieve her. Orchard's ship the America was thus delayed for 3 weeks. The deponent who was previously examined in **Saunders v. Orchard** came home in the Bonny Bess which carried a full freight.

Thomas Tilson of Ratcliffe, Middlesex, shipwright aged 33. He went to Virginia as carpenter of the America and returned home in the Bonny Bess.

William Atterbury of St. Andrew Undershaft, London, grocer aged 33. He went to Virginia in the America and returned in her to London. Hugh Weston had authority from Joseph Saunders to sell the Bonny Bess.

GREGORY CLEMENTS v. ----- YEO & HUMPHREY FARLEY.
17 August 1640 to 22 January 1640/41.

Luke Mariner of Stepney, Middlesex, mariner aged 30, deposes for Gregory Clements and Richard Shute. He joined the America as her commander on 20 October 1638 for a voyage to America at which time her owners were Humphrey Farley, Simon Turgess and Mr. Batson. A great sickness on board which caused the deaths of 37 persons obliged her to call at Bermuda from where she left in June 1639 for Virginia. Some 4 miles off the Virginia coast she came to anchor and beat against the wind for more than 3 months to reach land before giving up the attempt. She then headed for the West Indies to load and returned to Holland where the passengers refused to continue further because of the leakiness of the ship.

ENGLISH ADVENTURERS

Peter Rickforde of Wapping Wall, Middlesex, mariner aged 32. He served on the America of which the late Master was Alexander Caroe. She left from Dartmouth on 19 November 1638 bound for Virginia at which time her owners were Richard Batson, Thomas Norwoode, Humphrey Farley, Richard Wake, William Perry, one Mr. Sturges and one Mr. Sixtye of Virginia. She arrived at Bermuda on 19 May 1639. When she was within sight of Cape Henry, Virginia, she beat off shore until 1 November 1639 when few of her seamen were left alive and her provisions were almost exhausted.

Richard Surtis of Stepney, Middlesex, yeoman aged 33. (2 depositions). He went on the America as factor for Mr. Seely and Mr. Anthony to receive debts due to them in Virginia. When he first knew the ship in 1637 Robert Anderson was her Master and Alexander Caroe succeeded him.

Alexander Caro of Ratcliffe, Middlesex, mariner aged 35. (2 depositions). He first knew the America in 1637 in the Virginia River and kept a log of his voyages in her which is now (January 1640/41) in his custody aboard his ship the Elizabeth and Mary at Falmouth.

JOHN COUCHMAN v. JOHN BEALE. 29 July 1640.

Henry Beale of St. Giles, Cripplegate, London, salter aged 61. He was Master of the Falcon in which Maurice Thompson had a share and in 1629 sold a share in her to John Couchman. During 1630 and 1631 she made 3 voyages to Virginia and, after the last voyage, the deponent and Couchman brought suit against John Beale to secure their profit from the adventure.

——— WHITE v. JOSEPH SAUNDERS. 2 September 1640.

Thomas Wych of St. Mildred Poultry, London, aged 17. Joseph Saunders signed a deed at his house 3 months ago to the use of Captain Henry Saunders.

Daniel Saunders of St. Mildred Poultry, London, apprentice to Joseph Saunders, merchant, aged 20, deposes similarly.

JOHN STEVENS v. ——— SWANLY.
10 October to 21 December 1640.

Robert Price of St. Anne, Aldersgate, London, sailor aged 26. He went Master's mate to Virginia in the <u>Charity</u>, Mr. John Cole, which loaded tobacco and returned to London. Her owners were John Stevens, Waldrove Lodwicke, Edward Hopgood & Co. When the <u>Charity</u> attempted to moor in the Thames next to the <u>Jason</u>, Mr. Swanly, she ran ashore and her tobacco was damaged by wet.

Stephen Hawes of Wapping, Middlesex, sailor aged 40.

John Younge of Wapping, Middlesex, sailor aged 30.

Robert Buckingham of All Hallows on the Wall, London, silkweaver aged 62.

EDWARD HARRIS v. THE JANE. 20 October 1640.

Tobias Smith of Virginia, planter aged 25, deposes at the request of Edward Harris and Thomas Throgmorton, merchants. He viewed tobacco which had come from Virginia in the <u>Jane</u> and found most of it to be perishing.

Richard Bennington of St. Olave, Southwark, Surrey, porter aged 45.

Robert Roberts of St. Olave, Southwark, Surrey, silkweaver aged 59. In 1638 he was a porter and took tobacco from a lighter in the Thames to a warehouse on behalf of Harris and Throgmorton. The warehouse was then overflowed by water.

ENGLISH ADVENTURERS

----- JENKS & ----- BAYNES v. ----- SPINKARD.
22 January 1640/41.

George Sharrock of St. Bride, Fleet Street, London, aged 22 and under the tutelage of his mother. He went as a passenger to Providence in the Providence, Mr. Pinkard, and returned home in her as a cabin boy. From Providence the ship went to New England with passengers of whom Samuel Barton, Peter Talbot, Miles Bradford and Richard Beaton came away again in the ship while the others remained to trade tobacco. Pinkard remained for 7 weeks in New England to complete repairs to his leaky ship. On the return voyage Pinkard left the Providence when she arrived at Galloway, Ireland, and all the tobacco on board was left in the care of factors for Barton and Talbot. Philip Tayler transported a small quantity of tobacco home in the ship on his own account. The chief owners of the ship were John Wells and Samuel Barton who sold her when she reached Plymouth.

VOLUME 57

CRADDOCK, HARDEDGE & CO. v. ----- HAWKINS & ----- TAYLER. 12 & 13 May 1641.

Christopher Mills of Stepney, Middlesex, sailor aged 35. He went to New England as Master's mate of the 350 ton Mary Constance which left Gravesend on 7 August 1640 and arrived at Boston on 23 October following where she discharged goods and passengers to factors for Hawkins and Tayler.

Henry Barnes of St. Botolph, Aldgate, London, sailor aged 28. He went as boatswain of the ship (of 420 tons) which carried 80 passengers and goods to the account of Mr. Craddocke.

William Steede of Stepney, Middlesex, sailor aged 38. He went as gunner's mate of the ship (of 360 tons).

Andrew Johnson of Stepney, Middlesex, sailor aged

almost 30. He went as gunner of the Mary Constance which took passengers aboard at Gravesend and at the Downs.

----- HUBBERDSEY v. ----- PENNISTON.
3 July to 4 October 1641.

Thomas Tilson of Ratcliffe, Middlesex, sailor aged 32. In August 1640 he engaged on the Richard and Anne, Mr. Richard Ingle, for a voyage to Virginia for which the freighters were Penniston, Allen and others. When she arrived at St. Mary's "upon the sentinel of Virginia" she discharged goods into the care of John Lewgar in exchange for tobacco which was consigned to London for Captain Thomas Cornwallis, Mr. Edward Harris and the deponent.

William Kinge of Redriffe, Surrey, sailor aged 34. He went as boatswain of the ship.

John Smith of St. Gregory by St. Paul's, London, linen draper aged 44. When the Richard and Anne arrived back in London he received a letter from John Lewgar dated St. Mary's, 15 March 1640/41.

Edward Harris of St. Dunstan in the East, London, merchant aged 45. He received a letter from Lewgar dated St. Mary's, 16 March 1640/41, certifying that he had received the goods and passengers consigned to him.

VOLUME 58

UNIDENTIFIED CASE. 15 August 1642.

Captain Thomas Fitch of St. Giles in the Fields, Middlesex, aged 40. He was a passenger in the William and Sarah, Mr. James Morecock, which was driven on to rocks and lost 20 to 30 leagues out from Providence while on passage to Virginia. 50 or 60 souls were saved from her.

ENGLISH ADVENTURERS

JOHN COLE v. ----- JACKSON.
17 & 18 October 1642.

John Small of St. Botolph, Bishopsgate, London, sailor aged 30. He served on the Mayflower, Mr. John Cole, which left London with 140 passengers bound for Virginia. On 27 December 1641 while she was in the Downs the Magdalen, Mr. Hosier, came alongside at night to anchor and fouled the Mayflower's moorings.

Nicholas Wilbore of St. Katherine by the Tower, London, sailor aged 22, deposes similarly.

Robert Reeves of Ratcliffe, Middlesex, sailor aged 45, deposes similarly.

WILLIAM ALLEN v. HENRY PEIRCE.
26 November 1642.

Thwaits Pepper of Wapping, Middlesex, sailor aged 42. Henry Peirce was Master and part owner of the Elizabeth of which John Hutchins was also part owner and Master's mate. Peirce agreed with William Allen the younger for repairs to be carried out to the ship to prepare her for a voyage to Virginia.

John Nuttinge of Wapping, Middlesex, shipwright aged 50, deposes similarly.

Thomas Garland of Wapping, Middlesex, shipwright aged 40, deposes similarly.

RICHARD LATHAM & ----- PARKER v. JOHN JOHNSON. 1 to 9 June 1643.

George Fletcher of St. Dunstan in the East, London, where he has lived since birth, merchant aged 37. In 1640 the Unity, of which he is part owner, was freighted to Maurice Thompson, William Douglas, John Johnson and the deponent for a voyage to Virginia with passengers and goods.

ENGLISH ADVENTURERS

Matthew Graves of Limehouse, Middlesex, where he has lived from birth, shipwright aged 47. He was one of 7 owners of the Unity. She was at sea for 20 months on an ill voyage from which tobacco was lost.

William Douglas of St. Katherine, Coleman Street, London, where he has lived for 4 years, merchant aged 55. He went as Master of the Unity of which Richard Latham was a part owner. She was let in July 1640 to Maurice Thompson and others.

VOLUME 59

RANDALL MANWARINGE v. ----- DESSAREY.
17 February 1643/4 to 28 April 1645.

John Medlar of St. Mary at Hill, London, sailor aged 23. He served for 4 months in the Elizabeth, Mr. Benjamin Woolmer, of which Joseph Hawes was the owner. In 1637 she left London with 120 passengers and goods for Virginia but was surprised 250 leagues off the Virginia coast by 11 or 12 ships of the Spanish West Indian fleet and taken to Cadiz. In 1640 the Spanish Fleet set out from Cadiz for the West Indies under the command of the same General who had taken the Elizabeth but he was killed in an encounter with the French fleet and the Spaniards returned to Cadiz. A ship called the Santa Clara, Mr. Benedict Stafford, was in the Spanish fleet and a number of Englishmen who served in her left the ship at St. Domingo.

Diego Velio de Silva of Oporto, Portugal, gent aged 50. He served in the Spanish fleet and has taken the Oath of Supremacy to the Pope and the Oath of Allegiance to the King of Portugal. The Spanish fleet which seized the Elizabeth in 1637 was under the command of the Marques de Cardonozo.

Edward Rhodes of Poplar, Middlesex, sailor aged 33. (2 depositions). He is a Protestant of the Church of England and was Master's mate of the Elizabeth when she was captured. The passengers in her were dispersed to the Spanish ships, the men being separated from their wives. The commander of the Spanish fleet at that time was Signior Paulus de Conraves, a short man with a great pair of whiskers.

William Dalbye of St. Botolph, Billingsgate, London, weaver aged 37. He is a Protestant of the Church of England and has lived in Spain for 6 years. He was at Cadiz when the Elizabeth was brought there.

Lewis Jackson of St. Andrew Wardrobe, London, gent aged 56. He is a Roman Catholic of the Romish Church and has taken the Oath of Allegiance to the King but not the Oath of Supremacy. He has lived in Spain and knows the house in Seville which manages the Spanish West Indies fleet.

William Lowth of Deptford, Kent, shipwright aged 38. He is an English Protestant of the Church of England and was one of those taken from the Elizabeth by the Spanish fleet which was carrying silver, indigo and tobacco to Cadiz. The captives were treated very abusively.

John Nott of Stepney, Middlesex, shipwright aged 32. He is a Protestant of the Church of England and served as carpenter's mate of the Elizabeth.

William Bromhall of St. Gregory, London, mercer aged 64. He is a Protestant of the Church of England. He was for 2 years a journeyman to Nathaniel Hawes who in 1637 had a great trade in partnership with Randall Manwaring. On the death of Joseph Hawes they took out letters of administration to his estate.

Richard Burton of Ratcliffe, Middlesex, cooper aged 34. He is a Protestant of the Church of England. After his capture from the Elizabeth he was beaten almost every day by the Spaniards, some of whom were so unruly that they would have ravished the women passengers from the Elizabeth unless they had been prevented by their commanders. The deponent shipped home from Cadiz in an English vessel.

ENGLISH ADVENTURERS

(see also RE THE ELIZABETH, p. 90).

JOHN MARSTON v. THE HOPE. 23 August 1644.

Robert Anderson of Wapping, Middlesex, mariner aged 42. In 1636 he went from London to New England in the Hope which carried goods on behalf of John Marston, Edmond Cason & Co. and delivered them to Samuel Mavericke.
(HCA 23/14 contains a receipt for goods, mainly clothing, signed by Mavericke).

----- SNOWE v. THE RICHMOND. 26 November 1644.

Stephen Serjeant of Plymouth, Devon, sailor aged 36. He was Master of the Richmond whose owners were Robert Trelawney, deceased, and Mr. John Winter, a merchant resident in New England. On 25 March last Trelawney's factor at Lisbon loaded her with salt which was intended for Newfoundland but the factor directed her to go to Barnstaple which was then under the protection of the Parliament. The ship was seized and taken to London.

Tristram Bowes of Plymouth, Devon, sailor aged 50. He served on the Richmond.

RE THE MARY OF BRISTOL. 20 November 1644.

William Bowen of Bristol, mariner aged 23. He was boatswain's mate of the Mary, Mr. John Gwyn, which sailed to New England with a lading of coals, nails and other goods from Bristol in April 1644 when the city was in the hands of the King's forces. In New England she took a lading of fish known as Poor John, tobacco and wax to be carried to Bilbao, Cadiz, Mallaga and Bristol, but while she was at Charleston, New England she was surprized by the Bessie of London, Mr. Stagg. The owners of the Mary, William Cole, William Camm, Roger Bemstone, Dorothy Cole, widow, and one Wasbury, a cooper, all inhabitants of Bristol, have thereby suffered loss. At Christmas 1643 the Mary took prize a Dartmouth ship loaded with fish and brought her into Bristol.

John Read of Ashton near Bristol, sailor aged 20. He served in the Mary which was surprized by the Elizabeth, Captain Stagg. The Mary's owners were William Cole, Dorothy Cole, widow, Roger Bamston and one Nashbarrow, cooper, all of Bristol, and her freighters were Mr. Jackson and Mr. Browne, Bristol merchants.

John Davies of Bedminster near Bristol, sailor aged 19.

EDWARD GIBBONS v. WILLIAM COPELAND.
12 to 17 April 1645.

William Thomas of Carnarvon, Wales, gent aged 27. At Christmas 1644 a 50 ton vessel laden with tobacco and staves of which John Cutting was Master and Peregrine White the merchant was driven by accident into Carnarvon while she was on course from New England to Glasgow. She was owned by Edward Gibbons, Valentine Hill, David Yale and Thomas Fowle. She was seized at Carnarvon and renamed the Rupert of Beaumaris before being freighted by Captain Spicer from Ireland for voyages to France and Ireland under John Vaughan as Master. In France she was seized and brought into Portsmouth.

John Bishop of Newberry, New England, shipwright aged 24. He was one of the company of John Cutting's ship, the Adventure, which was forced into Carnarvon by bad weather and was there declared forfeit to the King. The ship was built in Plymouth, New England. Captain Spicer bore arms against the Parliament.

John Gallopp of Boston, New England, sailor aged 27. The owners of the Adventure were all inhabitants of Boston and her company, also from Boston, were John Bishop her carpenter, a Scotsman named James her boatswain, John Copp and one named Francis common men, and not more than 8 others.

VOLUME 60 - UNFIT FOR PRODUCTION

VOLUME 61

ROGER LAWRENCE v. GILES WEBB.
20 to 21 April 1649.

John Watson of Ratcliffe, Middlesex, sailor aged 41. In October 1648 the John and Isaac, of which Roger Lawrence was Master and part owner, was loaded with tobacco in Virginia by Giles Webb and William Scott who came home in her. On 28 February 1648/9 she met with a violent storm and, to prevent her sinking, some of the tobacco was thrown overboard.

The following depose similarly:

Frederick Johnson of Wapping, Middlesex, sailor aged 37.

John Irish of St. Botolph, Aldgate, London, sailor aged 36.

Robert Cannon of St. Katherine by the Tower, London, sailor aged 30.

William Zanes of Stepney, Middlesex, sailor aged 30.

RE THE PROSPEROUS SUSAN. 8 to 11 June 1649.

Nathaniel Cooke of Ipswich, Suffolk, mariner aged 38, deposes for Jonathan Gibbs. He was Master of the Prosperous Susan which left London on 12 August 1648 and arrived in Charles River, Virginia, at the end of October. On her return voyage she was driven by adverse winds on to the rocks at Scilly on 29 March 1649 and was utterly lost.

John Jucie of Wapping, Middlesex, mariner aged 26. He was Master's mate of the Prosperous Susan.

ENGLISH ADVENTURERS

----- FREER v. ----- MEERS.   31 May 1649.

John Fox of St. Botolph without Aldgate, London, sailor aged 27. He was boatswain of the <u>William and George</u> which sprang a leak on her homeward voyage from Virginia by which her tobacco was damaged.

VOLUME 62

FOR HOLLAND WEST INDIES COMPANY.
8 October to 16 December 1647 (<u>sic</u>).

Lawrence van Heusden of Oudtbeyrland, Holland, aged 47, a servant of the Holland West Indies Company at New Netherlands.   In May 1647 the <u>Princes</u> of Amsterdam commanded by John Clauson Boll came from Carsowe in the West Indies carrying wood and skins from the New Netherlands in Virginia. While still on course for Amsterdam she was cast away on 27 September 1647 about 8 miles from Swansea off the coast of Wales and her whole company except for 21 persons were lost.   A great part of her cargo was washed ashore where it was looted.

Henry Ellerre of Carsoer, Denmark, merchant aged 24. He is a factor for the Netherlands West India Company and survived the shipwreck.

John Clauson Boll of Amsterdam, mariner aged 25.   He was Captain of the <u>Princes</u>.

William Jones of Amsterdam, aged 40.   He is a servant of the Holland West India Company and was returning home on the <u>Princes</u>.

----- EVERING v. JOHN FOCHE & WILLIAM HATLEY.
18 March 1649/50.

Edmund Leach of St. Matthew, Friday Street, London, where he has resided for 3 months, merchant aged 32. He went passenger in the <u>Swallow</u>, Mr. Greene, in

March 1647/8 to Boston, New England, where he sold goods loaded in that ship and in the Chapman, Mr. Preice, for the account of John Foche and William Hatley.

THOMAS SMITH v. JOHN STONE. 8 to 11 April 1650.

William Lea of Shadwell, Stepney, Middlesex, sailor aged 33. He was boatswain of the Pilgrim alias Peregrine of London, Mr. Thomas Hawkins, for a voyage to New England. When Hawkins died on passage the chief mate, John Stone, succeeded him for the rest of the voyage back to London via Naples, Messina and Alexandria. (This case concerns payments to the ship's company and Stone's alleged cruelties).

Francis Hammond of Shadwell, Stepney, Middlesex, sailor aged 24. He served on the ship which was chartered in August 1648 by Thomas Smith. (Vol. 63).

Josias Church of Shadwell, Stepney, Middlesex, sailor aged 27. He was hired in New England to serve on the ship's return voyage to London. (Vol. 63).

GEORGE REYMOND v. ROBERT BOURNE.
JOSEPH POTTER & JOHN SMITH v. GEORGE REYMOND.
8 May to 20 November 1650.

Robert Chamberlaine of Wapping, Middlesex, sailor aged 57. He was a quartermaster of the Eagle which on her outward voyage from London loaded salt at Lisbon for New England and then went on to James Town and Nancy Mum River, Virginia. There she loaded tobacco to the accounts of Robert Bourne, William Painter, Mr. Potter, Robert Clarke, John Wingfield, John Rice, Thomas Potts and Humfrey Owen. On her homeward passage about 150 leagues from Virginia the Eagle ran into a great storm in March 1650 and another at the end of the same month off Scilly as the result of which she sprang a great leak which damaged her tobacco.

ENGLISH ADVENTURERS

Gilbert Lilley of Ipswich, Suffolk, shipwright aged 39. The Eagle, Mr. George Reymond, sailed from Virginia on 23 February 1649/50 carrying tobacco for Robert Bourne, John Boswell, William Painter and others.

Robert Cawley of Redriffe, Surrey, where he has been resident for 5 years, sailor aged 51.

Richard Ryemond of Redriffe, Surrey, sailor aged 61. He was Master's mate of the Eagle.

Andrew Painter of Wapping, Middlesex, sailor aged 26. He has always been a seaman. He heard the carpenter of the Eagle say she was always a weak ship. She was loaded in Virginia at the same time as the Dragon, a vessel of smaller capacity. (Vol. 63).

John Turner of St. Benet Finck, London, citizen and fishmonger of London aged 64. Thomas Potter, one of the plaintiffs, asked him and Joseph Potter to appraise the tobacco which arrived in London on the Eagle in May 1650. (Vol. 63).

Joseph Potter of All Saints the Less, London, grocer aged 22. He appraised the tobacco carried by the Eagle including that claimed by John Smith and Laurence Steele. (Vol. 63).

Roger Jeffreys of St. Antholin, London, apprentice of Thomas Potter, aged 22. He examined damaged tobacco belonging to William Parker and Samuel Jourdaine. Tobacco of the same quality as that carried in the Eagle was sold by Richard Preston to Mr. Richard Abbot of London, merchant. (Vol. 63).

VOLUME 63

RE THE PETER AND JOHN. 25 May 1650.

Thomas Byam of the Liberty of the Tower of London, mariner aged 46, deposes for John White, merchant and grocer whom he has known for 4 years. He was

Master's mate of the Peter and John, Mr. Nathaniel Cooke, which arrived in Virginia in September 1649. She was loaded with tobacco at Charles River in January 1649/50 by Francis Wheeler and his factor Thomas Ramsey but it was damaged on the homeward voyage when the ship met with bad weather.

Robert Jones of St. Saviour, Southwark, Surrey, mariner aged 22.

HUGH LOCKYER v. JOHN LOCKYER.
20 August to 23 September 1650.

John Lockyer of Limehouse, Stepney, Middlesex, mariner aged ?30.   On 13 September 1649 he went as Master of the William and Ralph alias the Virginia Merchant on a voyage to Virginia.   On 13 November, when she was 14 leagues from Hatteras, she met a great storm in which she was severely damaged and on reaching James River, Virginia, was declared a wreck.

Thomas Stanton of Ratcliffe, Middlesex, mariner aged 26.   He went as a Master's mate of the ship.

John Skinner of Ratcliffe, Stepney, Middlesex, sailor aged 30.   He went as a Master's mate of the Virginia Merchant for which voyage Hugh Lockyer, Edward Wood, George Spurgin, Richard Payne, Nicholas Paddock and Thomas Reason were also hired in September 1649. Hugh Lockyer and George Spurgin were disobedient during the voyage.

Philip Stephens of St. James, Duke's Place, London, merchant aged 28.   He was a passenger in the ship and carried freight in her.   John Lockyer was paid in Virginia for his other passengers and freight.   The Virginia Merchant was left as a wreck in Virginia in March 1649/50.

George Putt of Shadwell, Middlesex, sailor aged 42.   He also went as a Master's mate on the Virginia Merchant.

ENGLISH ADVENTURERS

EDWARD ARLABEER & ----- BEST v. ----- JANCEY.
JOHN BARDWELL & HENRY TROTT v. -----
COLEMAN. 14 October 1650 to 23 January 1650/51.

John Harrison of St. Katherine by the Tower, London, sailor aged 40. He has gone to sea from his youth and engaged on the <u>Jonathan and Abigail</u> for a voyage to Barbados and Virginia under Captain Robert Page and Master and part-owner Adam Groves. During that voyage she proved leaky, her freight and victuals were damaged by water, and it was generally believed that she had not been well caulked after a previous voyage to Newcastle. After discharging her passengers and goods at Barbados the ship went on to Virginia where she had to be recaulked and thereby lost time and return freight.

John Baldwin of St. Katherine by the Tower, London, sailor aged 33. He has been to sea for 12 months and in 1643 went to Virginia in the <u>William and George,</u> Mr. Babb. The wages of the <u>Jonathan and Abigail</u>'s company were paid by Mr. Jancey. On her outward voyage the ship was so awash that the passengers and company could not lie down: this and the want of provisions occasioned the death of 36 passengers and 12 seamen. Had these passengers reached Barbados alive they might have fetched 500 weight of sugar. In Virginia the ship's company spent much time cutting down trees in order to make tar for caulking, and when ships arrived there from New England they were forced to trade with them for provisions. The climate is so hot at Barbados, and the heat of the sun so great, that it will melt a ship's pitch and shrink her planks.

John Ley of Shadwell, Middlesex, sailor aged 34. He has been to sea for 23 years and was gunner's mate of the <u>Jonathan and Abigail.</u> The delays incurred at Barbados and Virginia extended the ship's voyage by 9 months. On her outward passage her 2 carpenters died and there was none on the voyage from Barbados to Virginia and only one from Virginia back to Barbados.

Henry Twisell of Shadwell, Middlesex, sailor aged 34.

He has been to sea for 22 years, for 15 of them as an officer, and was gunner of the Jonathan and Abigail. Her freighters paid for the building of cabins for the 250 or 260 passengers she carried from England. She arrived at Virginia in April 1649 intending to load cattle for Barbados.

Phillip Davies of Limehouse, Middlesex, shipwright aged 30. He has been a ship carpenter for 8 or 9 years. Robert Page hired him in Virginia as carpenter of the Jonathan and Abigail and 3 other carpenters were hired to work on her for a month. Edward Arlabeer and Mr. Best were the owners of the ship.

John Tilley of St. Botolph, Aldgate, London, sailor aged 30. (2 depositions). He has been to sea for 17 years and was engaged as boatswain of the Jonathan and Abigail by Adam Graves who went as Master but who died on passage. In April and May cattle in Virginia are commonly fat. While she was in Barbados on her return voyage sugars were loaded for John Austerlie.

Roger Smith of Ratcliffe, Middlesex, sailor aged 28. He has been to sea for 12 years, engaged as a cooper on the Jonathan and Abigail but was then made a Master's mate.

William Hurler of Wapping, Middlesex, caulker aged 38. The Jonathan and Abigail was built as a collier for the Newcastle trade and he worked on her after her return to London from Newcastle in 1648, but Robert Page discharged the caulkers before they had completed their work.

William Benger of Ratcliffe, Middlesex, shipwright aged 32. He was hired as the ship's carpenter and converted her for passenger use, taking away her hatches and replacing them with gratings. He was once in Virginia where he stayed for 14 months. He knows the inhabited parts well and found the climate to be as temperate there as it is in England. No commodities except cattle and victuals are customarily carried from Virginia to Barbados. In April the cattle in Virginia are very poor and lean after the extremity of winter so that many can scarcely rise after lying down: they are not fat or ready to be killed until the end of June.

Robert Moyer of Leigh, Essex, sailor aged 29. He was a Master's mate of the ship which discharged in London on 11 September 1650. While she was in Virginia her company cut down pine trees intending to make tar but then bought what was needed from Thomas Marshe, a planter there, for which they paid him in mollasses.

Robert Trundle of Wapping, Middlesex, shipwright aged 32. He helped to build the ship at Woodbridge, Suffolk, and worked on her after her return from Newcastle.

Thomas Garner of Wapping, Middlesex, sailor aged 41. He joined the ship in Barbados after she had returned there from Virginia.

Christopher Sedgwick of Wapping, Middlesex, citizen and clothworker of London aged 55. He is by profession a shipwright and caulker and worked on the ship after her return from Newcastle.

Giles Sisson of Wapping, Middlesex, caulker aged 40. He worked on the ship after her return from Newcastle.

William Lovell of Wapping, Middlesex, shipwright aged 31. He worked on the ship both in Newcastle and in London.

Captain Thomas Willoughby of Willoughby's Hope, Norfolk County, Virginia, gent aged 52. He has lived in Virginia for 39 years and came from there at the beginning of March 1649/50. He was in Virginia when the Jonathan and Abigail arrived there at the beginning of April 1649 when he was Lieutenant of the County of Nether Norfolk. Captain Robert Page came often to his house and blamed the defects of his ship on the heat of the weather. He laid out a considerable amount of tobacco to pay the carpenters who worked on her.

ENGLISH ADVENTURERS

Richard Jennings of Bermuda, merchant aged 51. He was factor for John Bardwell and Henry Trott and on their behalf loaded sugars on to the Jonathan and Abigail in April 1650.

John Sutcole of Ratcliffe, Middlesex, shipwright aged 63. He was hired to convert the ship to carry passengers. (Vol. 64).

William Sutcole of Poplar, Middlesex, shipwright aged 57, brother of the above, deposes similarly. (Vol. 64).

Humphrey Smallwood of All Saints the Greater, London, merchant aged 22. He was with Robert Page 17 days before his death and received from him a Bill of Lading for sugars dated Carlisle Bay, Barbados, 10 June 1649. (Vol. 64).

VOLUME 64

DOUGLAS BURTON v. THOMAS VARVELL 6 ROBERT LLEWELLIN. 7 December 1650 to 10 January 1650/51.

John Dustin of Wapping, Middlesex, sailor aged 40. Thomas Varvell and Robert Llewellin hired him as cook, William Burton as surgeon and Philip Cooper as surgeon's mate for a voyage to Virginia in the Increase. After the ship had arrived in Bermuda and discharged some of her passengers and goods Burton died, having served from September to December 1648. He was buried in Bermuda and his place was taken by Cooper. It is usual for passengers to Virginia to pay 2s 6d a head to the surgeon "for all the harm of the voyage" so that he will care for them in case of any sickness or mischance. This is in addition to what the surgeon receives in wages and has been a customary practice on all the 5 voyages the deponent has made to Virginia. Burton had a woman servant on board the Increase named Susanna May and she was sold in Bermuda by Varvell after Burton's death.

John Rose of Ratcliffe, Middlesex, sailor aged 19. He

was a steward on the ship which carried 260 passengers. Cooper served on the ship until her return to London in July 1649.

Richard Murdue of Poplar, Middlesex, sailor aged 26. Cooper was skilled as a surgeon and was aged about 22.

Marin de Lamondasse of St. Giles, Cripplegate, London, surgeon aged 42. He had accompanied Burton on 2 voyages and has made several voyages to Virginia himself. If a passenger refuses to pay 2s 6d to the surgeon he is liable to be compelled by the ship's Master.

Thomas Bell of St. Giles, Cripplegate, London, surgeon aged 26. He knows the plaintiff Douglas Burton to be the relict of William Burton and was present when Cooper bound himself as apprentice to Burton.

Lancelot Coxon of Limehouse, Middlesex, surgeon aged 48. He has made 5 voyages to Virginia and on each occasion received 2s 6d for each passenger.

John Bowney of St. Saviour, Southwark, Surrey, surgeon aged 32. He bought the Increase's medicine chest on her return to London and paid only £3 for it as it was so washed and spoiled. Merchants and Masters of ships sometimes pay 2s 6d for those passengers who are poor or are servants.

Robert Ridley of Ratcliffe, Middlesex, waterman aged 37. He was employed by Burton to carry his goods aboard the Increase.

Richard Cawthorne of St. Mildred Poultry, London, citizen and stationer of London aged ?31. After the return of the Increase to London he went with Douglas Burton to Thomas Varvall's house in Ratcliffe to demand an account of her husband's goods. She had taken out letters of administration to her husband's estate.

RE THE MARY OF LONDON.
31 December 1650 to 5 June 1651.

ENGLISH ADVENTURERS

Leonard Guy of Redriffe, Surrey, shipwright aged 50. He worked on the Mary for 1 month before she sailed for Virginia in 1648, a voyage for which she was well fitted.

Daniel Gardner of Limehouse, Middlesex, mariner aged 32. He was cook of the Mary, Mr. William Thomas, and served on her for 5 years. On her outward passage to Virginia she ran into storms and suffered damage. He returned from Virginia in another ship while the Mary was detained in New England for repairs.

George Stapleton of Charterhouse, St. Bartholomew the Great, London, mariner aged 18. He kept the account books of the Mary in which he noted the repairs done in New England.

John Dennis of Limehouse, Middlesex, mariner aged 32. The Mary was a stout ship and he has been her gunner for 7 years.

RE THE DILIGENCE OF BOSTON, NEW ENGLAND.
3 February 1650/51.

Robert Henfield of Boston, New England, mariner aged 28. He, Joseph Grafton of Salem, New England, and William Andrewes of Cambridge, New England,. were owners of the Diligence which was taken off Cape Cod by French men of war while she was on a trading voyage along the coast of New England carrying linen and strong waters. The ship's company were set ashore on an uninhabited island where they were left to fend for themselves while their ship was taken to St. John's in the Bay of Fundy.

Roland Bevan of Boston, New England, mariner aged 26. He was in company with the Diligence in the William of Boston which was bound for the West Indies. When he returned to Boston he found the ship's company of the Diligence had returned to that town after their ship had been captured. The Diligence was built at Salem, New England, 10 years ago.

ENGLISH ADVENTURERS

Nicholas Trewergy of Piscatoqua, New England, sailor aged 22. He served on the <u>Diligence</u>.

Henry Parke of St. Matthew, Friday Street, London, mariner aged 25. He lived in Boston, New England, for 6 years until October 1650 and remembers the taking of the <u>Diligence</u> in 1645. In November 1648 his boat was driven by foul weather into St. John's River where he saw the <u>Diligence</u> in the possession of the French.

ROBERT RICHE v. PERCIVAL WESTON.
8 February 1650/51.

William White of Shadwell, Middlesex, sailor aged 46. He went as boatswain of the <u>Speedwell</u>, Mr. Diggory Curwithie, of which the owners were Percival Weston & Co., for a voyage to New England. Because the ship was leaky she let water between New England and the Canaries, her cargo was spoiled, and merchants in New England refused to load her with goods or passengers for the homeward voyage. Her carpenter, John Collison, informed George Butcher that the ship's decks were uncaulked.

Stephen Baxter of Wapping, Middlesex, sailor aged 56.

Thomas Brookes of Ratcliffe, Middlesex, sailor aged 35.

PHILIP ALLEN & LUKE LUCYE v. WILLIAM WOODLAND.
THOMAS DAY v. JOHN GIBBS.
7 March 1650/51 to 7 December 1651.

William Shuckborowe of St. Olave, Southwark, Surrey, waterman aged 57. He was cook of the <u>Constant Luke</u>, Mr. John Gibbs of which the owners were Luke Lucye and Philip Allen. In October 1648 she sailed from Gravesend on a voyage to the West Indies and New England, returning by way of Barbados and Dublin to London. The Master's mate, William Woodland, a stubborn, headstrong man, prevented the ship from going to New England whereby she incurred great loss. On her homeward voyage she was taken by a privateer to the Scilly Isles where she was despoiled and the deponent was imprisoned for 5 months. The Constant Luke returned to London in February 1650/51.

John Gibbs of St. Olave, Southwark, Surrey, mariner aged 47. He was hired by Thomas Day to go Master of the Constant Luke and departed from London on 22 October 1648. After she had left the Western Isles David Wrangham and others of the ship's company coerced him by threats, including throwing a live hog overboard, not to proceed to New England but to go direct to Bermuda. (Vol. 65).

RE THE CHAPMAN OF LONDON. 26 March 1651.

Thomas Kemble of Charles Town, New England, merchant aged 30. In 1650 he, Francis Norton, Nicholas Davidson and John Paris, merchants of New England, freighted the Chapman, Mr. Nicholas Trevize (Twisse), from her owner Robert Rich for a voyage from New England to Madeira and return. She was loaded with pipestaves in May 1650 and arrived in July at Madeira where she was taken by the Portuguese. The deponent was Rich's factor in New England and had voyaged to London and back in the Chapman.

John Cooke of London, servant of Robert Rich, aged 17. He has seen a copy of the charter party for the voyage.

Samuel Mantle of London, servant of Robert Rich, aged 19. He went in the Chapman as Rich's agent and was responsible for paying for provisions.

FOR EDWARD GIBBONS. 7 May 1651.

Edward Winslowe of Marshfield in the Government of New Plymouth, New England, Esq aged 56. He was in New England when M. de la Torre built a fort in the northern parts on St. John's River which he and his men maintained at their own expense on a warrant from the French King. De la Torre went to Major-General Edward Gibbons and to the other principal English officers in the plantation seeking their help to defend the fort against M. de Aulney and mortgaged the fort in exchange for money. After the mortgage had been taken out de Aulney stirred up the French in 1640, 1641 and 1642, alleging that de la Torre was a heretic who had joined with the English in Protestant worship. He then captured the fort and put all the Englishmen there to the sword.

John Richards of Boston, New England, merchant aged 26. He has lived in New England for 19 years and was there when M. de la Torre the elder built the fort.

WILLIAM MOORE v. ROBERT LLEWELLIN.
24 May to 5 June 1651.

William Sheares of London, merchant aged 27. He went as supercargo of the Comfort, Mr. William Garnet, for a voyage to Virginia with passengers and goods. Four passengers paid £20 passage money and the others were carried at similar rates. Two weeks after leaving Plymouth the ship sprang leaks and her Master died soon after reaching Virginia. She loaded tobacco for Bannan Mackerell and the deponent's father Abraham Sheares and left Virginia for home in April 1650.

Thomas Chinn of Shadwell, Middlesex, mariner aged 35. He succeeded William Garnet as Master.

George Putt of Shadwell, Middlesex, mariner aged 41. Mr. William Sheares engaged him for the voyage and he spent 30 days repairing the ship at Warwicks Queake in Virginia.

Alexander Eve of St. Katherine near the Tower, London, wine cooper aged 50. He trimmed wine casks for the ship.

ENGLISH ADVENTURERS

Edward Nelson, Deputy Marshal of the Admiralty Court, aged 46. He issued warrants to William Moore and George Potts as part owners of the Comfort. Other part owners are Mr. Buckley of Tower Hill, London, and Anthony Hasselfe of Ipswich.

John Whales of St. Katherine by the Tower, London, gent aged 57. He witnessed the agreement made between the owners and freighters of the Comfort at the Cardinal's Cap in Cornhill, London.

Maurice Henchman of All Hallows, Barking, London, citizen and skinner of London and Custom House officer and Surveyor of landwaiters, aged 53. In March 1651 by order of the Commissioners of Customs he and Elias Palmer surveyed the tobaccos damaged in the Comfort.

John Turner of St. Benet Finck, London, fishmonger aged 64. He is a sworn broker by profession and used to dealing in tobacco. He and John Wiche examined the tobacco on the Comfort.

William Hough of St. Lawrence Jewry, London, citizen and merchant tailor of London aged 28. He trades in the buying and selling of Virginia tobacco and has bought tobacco from Llewellin.

Thomas Taylor of Wapping, Middlesex, shipwright aged 47. He is a master carpenter and worked on the Comfort for 3 weeks before she left for Virginia. At that time she was a stout ship.

John Wadmer of Wapping, Middlesex, shipwright aged 56. He worked on the ship with Thomas Taylor.

Richard West of Wapping, Middlesex, caulker aged 40. He also worked on the ship before her voyage.

RE THE PETER BONADVENTURE OF LONDON. 28 June 1651.

John Jake of East Smithfield, London, mariner aged 26,

deposes for Christopher Willoughby re assurance on the Peter Bonadventure which loaded salt at Anguilla to be carried to Virginia but whose freight was damaged by leaks in the ship.

----- DAVISON & ----- LUCYE v. ----- JOHNSON & WILLIAM STEVENSON. 1 July 1651.

Philip Holton of Ipswich, Suffolk, mariner aged 30. He was hired by Abraham Child, boatswain of the Eagle, Mr. William Stevenson, to serve in the ship which sailed in staunch condition in April 1648 from the River Orwell to Nantes, France, where she loaded goods for New England. She arrived there in October 1648 after encountering many storms on passage. She was then recaulked and loaded fish to be taken to Bilbao but on the way was again overtaken by storms and put into St. Sebastian where her fish was unloaded. John Maverick, who was put into the ship by her merchants, left her at Plymouth: and Christopher Langley, William Talbot and several others left her at New England. She had been freighted by Davison, Lucye, Allen and Childe.

VOLUME 65

RE THE MARY OF LONDON. 14 October 1651.

Richard Mounteney of the Tower Precinct, London, aged 38.   When the Mary, Mr. Thomas Severne, went to Virginia in 1648 her owners were: the deponent who helped build her and kept her books; William Thomas who also helped to build her and who acquired a share from the deponent's brother Cornelius Mounteney; Mary Shotton as the relict of Robert Adams who also helped to build her; and John Dennis. The deponent also knew William Allen, now deceased.

Henry Roach of Wapping, Middlesex, shipwright aged 48.

ELIAS JOURDAINE & HENRY WEST v. RICHARD BATTSON. 8 to 28 January 1651/2.

ENGLISH ADVENTURERS

John Skinner of Ratcliffe, Middlesex, mariner aged 50. He is part owner of the William and Ralph, Mr. John Lockyer, and went in her as Master's mate for a voyage to Virginia. She was a stout ship of 280 tons and left Gravesend on 26 August 1649 in company with 2 other English ships bound for Virginia. But because she was under victualled she had to part company from the fleet to take on fresh provisions in the Western Isles after her passengers had suffered great hardship, sickness and mortality. Because of this delay the ship did not arrive off Cape Hatteras until the winter. This is a place where ships rarely venture except by accident because of the many shoals and sands there. The ship was driven on to the rocks and badly damaged though her goods and passengers, whose freight had been paid by Messrs. Batson, Jauncey, Austin and Lockyer, were safely put ashore.

John Lockyer went away from his ship and discharged her company having first taken some of the ship's furniture and sold it. The deponent, having been unable to obtain money to make repairs in Virginia, abandoned the ship there and took back her sails and 18 guns to England.

Richard Chubb of Limehouse, Middlesex, mariner aged 44. Cape Hatteras is considered a dangerous place.

Francis Turley of the Precinct of the Tower of London, cooper aged 36. He went as a passenger on the William and Ralph and it was ignorance on the part of her Master or pilot that took her to Cape Hatteras.

Philip Stevens of St. James, Duke's Place, London, Esq aged 29. He went as a passenger in the ship after having examined her diligently. She was abandoned in Virginia 7 months after her departure from England and her passengers were put ashore amongst the barbarous Moors and constrained to continue to Virginia overland. The deponent was a witness when John Lockyer was tried on a charge of starving his passengers.

(see also **LOCKYER v. LOCKYER,** p. 120).

NATHANIEL JESSON v. ABRAHAM READ. JOHN WILSON & ABRAHAM READ v. NATHANIEL JESSON. 25 July 1652 to 2 December 1653.

John Jasperson of Middleborough, Zealand, mariner aged 35. (Several depositions). He was Master of the Golden Lion owned by Peter de Leeun, Govert Lachard and others dwelling in the Spanish Dominions in Flanders. In August 1651 she set out from Amsterdam bound for Virginia carrying strong waters, clothing and shoes, arriving in James River in the following October. On 7 February 1651/2, before Virginia was brought under obedience to the Commonwealth in March 1651/2, she was seized by a fleet of 3 English ships, the William and John, Mr. Nathaniel Jesson, the Seven Sisters, Mr. Abraham Read, and the Charles, Mr. John Wilson. Several Virginia planters who had loaded their tobacco on the Golden Lion brought claims certified by Richard Bennett, Governor of Virginia, and William Cleborne, Commissioner of the Parliament for the plantation, which are now before the Admiralty Court.

Nicholas Smith who had shipped 30 hogsheads was in Amsterdam 3 months before the Golden Lion set out for Virginia and took passage in her with his wife. He was an Englishman well affected to the Parliament who had expressed his dislike of the enemies standing against them, and, should their cause have triumphed, had arranged to return to Amsterdam in the same ship.

John Bishop had 17 hogsheads of tobacco loaded in the ship on his behalf by Mr. Thomas Mason, a resident in Virginia.

Samuel Hart, an Englishman by birth dwelling in Virginia and a man well affected to the Commonwealth, loaded 10 hogsheads.

Giles Webb, an Englishman by birth living in Virginia, had a family and a plantation there and was well affected to the Commonwealth. When he loaded his tobacco in the Golden Lion there was only one other ship in James River or in any other part of Virginia bound for London, (the West India Merchant), apart from one which had already been fully loaded and was bound for Bristol. After the Golden Lion was seized Giles Webb had therefore to take passage from Virginia to London in a New England vessel but she was seized by the French and taken to St. Malo where Webb was kept prisoner.

Thomas Mason late of Virginia but now living on Tower Hill, London, merchant aged 52. Nicholas Smith had dwelt in Virginia for 26 years and was well affected to the Parliament, having spoken against the former power in Virginia and refused to take up arms in their cause. He loaded tobacco on the Golden Lion on account of Abraham de Leinn in Amsterdam, a man accounted to be an Englishman born in Yarmouth. John Bishop was an English born man who had been an inhabitant of Virginia for 22 years. Such was his affection to the Parliament that he would have removed himself with his wife and family from Virginia had the plantation not been reduced to the Parliamentary cause. The deponent had married Bishop's daughter.

William Young of Leith, Scotland, mariner aged 22. He served on the Golden Lion, a ship of 200 tons which carried 27 men and 15 guns and which was seized near Pegan Creek.

Matthias Johnson Jansen of Amsterdam but born at Cullen, sailor aged 28. (2 depositions). He served on the Golden Lion and took a sloop to Chuckatuck Creek to collect tobacco from John White.

Jacob Saunders of Middleborough in Zealand, mariner aged 48. He was steersman of the Golden Lion and well knows John Brown who came aboard with his tobacco.

John Martens of Middleborough in Zealand, sailor aged 20. He was purser of the ship and knows that John Brown owned a sloop that was seized.

ENGLISH ADVENTURERS

William Gill of Whitechapel, Middlesex, mariner aged 50. He was a quartermaster of the William and John which anchored at Newport News, Virginia, and seized a Dutch sloop at Chuckatuck Creek belonging to John Brown being used to deliver tobacco to the Golden Lion.

Edward Pharo of Ratcliffe, Middlesex, mariner aged 35. He was a quartermaster of the William and John

Jacob Marquez of Amsterdam, mariner aged 27. He was one of the company of the Golden Lion.

John Thurmer of St. Katherine by the Tower, London, planter aged 55. Giles Webb was a merchant who traded frequently to London and was a Burgess in Virginia. The deponent has known him for 17 years and was first a servant to him in Virginia.

John Price of St. Katherine by the Tower, London, Master of the West India Merchant, aged 30. He has frequent trade with Virginia and has known Giles Webb, who was born in Hampshire, for 8 years. The deponent returned to London in company with the Golden Lion at the same time as Webb left Virginia in a New England ship.

John Byrom of Virginia, planter aged 38. John Brown was a constant trader with Holland and the deponent was captured in his sloop.

William Ingleton of Wayne Oake on Charles River, Virginia, planter aged 31. Brown's sloop had been brought out of Holland and the deponent was aboard her in May 1652.

Giles Webb of Upper Northfolke, Virginia, planter aged 38. John Brown came to Virginia as merchant of the Golden Dolphin on behalf of Mr. James Deham of Rotterdam and had since made another voyage to Holland.

Thomas Stagg of St. Katherine by the Tower, London,

merchant aged 21. When he was living in Virginia he saw Dutchmen bring in materials for building a sloop.

Benjamin Osborne of St. Peter le Poer, London, merchant aged 19. He has known John Brown for several years and dwelt with him at Rotterdam from 1650 to 1652; both were born in North Yarmouth. In 1649 the Golden Lion belonged to James De Ham who was born at Norwich of English parents, and to Richard Ford who was born at Exeter. Tobias De Ham, also born at Norwich, brother of James De Ham, kept the ship's books.

Richard Ford of the City of London, merchant aged 38. He and James De Ham bought the Golden Lion at Rotterdam 5 years ago. He has known John Brown for 6 years.

James Sands of St. Botolph, Billingsgate, London, citizen and leatherseller of London, aged 27. John Brown, whom he has known for 20 years, was well affected to the Parliament and had served at sea with Captain Abraham Wheeler and others in the service of the Commonwealth.

Robert Williams of St. Michael, Wood Street, London, mariner aged 50. He has known John Brown for 16 years and has served under him at sea in the Commonwealth service since 1642.

Christopher Evelyng of Ratcliffe, Middlesex, mariner aged 26. He was boatswain of the William and John and was put in as Master's mate of the Golden Lion which he brought down the Virginia River where her company were put on shore before being taken on board the Seven Sisters, the Charles, and the William and John to be brought to England.

George Clements of Stepney, Middlesex, mariner aged 25. He served on the William and John.

John Staveley of Limehouse, Middlesex, mariner aged 23. He served on the William and John.

ENGLISH ADVENTURERS

Seger de Hem of St. Bartholomew near the Exchange, London, merchant aged 29. His brother James de Hem, an Englishman born in Norwich who had lived in Holland for many years, bought timber in Rotterdam and sent it out in a Dutch ship to Virginia where it was to be made up into a sloop for John Brown who was James de Hem's factor there.

William Cotton of All Hallows, Barking, London, merchant aged 21. He was in Rotterdam in October 1652 and heard witnesses depose there as to the seizure of the Golden Lion.

Thomas Wills of Ratcliffe, Middlesex, mariner aged 29. He was chief mate of the Seven Sisters commanded by Abraham Read. The plunder from the Golden Lion was divided between the Captains of the 3 English ships present.

Richard Lowe of the City of London, merchant aged 18. He went as a passenger to Virginia in the William and John.

Thomas Pott of Stepney, Middlesex, mariner aged 28. He commanded the John and Thomas which arrived in Virginia after the Golden Lion had been seized and when Mr. Byam had been installed as her Master. She was a ship of 200 tons and carried 18 guns and was seized at the same time as 2 other ships then in Virginia, the Peacock seized by Captain John Wilson, and the Charity seized by Captain Abraham Read. (Vol. 67).

James Wilson of Wapping, Middlesex, mariner aged 36. He was second mate of the Charles, Mr. Thomas Wilson. (Vol. 68).

Samuel Gardner of Ratcliffe, Middlesex, mariner aged 48. He was gunner of the Charles. (Vol. 68).

Lawrence Thompson of Ratcliffe, Middlesex, mariner aged 34. He was boatswain of the Charles. (Vol. 68).

ENGLISH ADVENTURERS

Titus Waimouth of Stepney, Middlesex, mariner aged 30. He was boatswain of the <u>Seven Sisters.</u> (Vol. 68).

Richard Tucker of Limehouse, Middlesex, aged 30. He was carpenter of the <u>Seven Sisters.</u> (Vol. 68).

RE THE FAME OF ROTTERDAM.
3 October to 4 November 1652.

Miles Cooke of St. Olave, Southwark, Surrey, mariner aged 28. He was Master's mate of the <u>Hopeful Adventure</u> of which the Master and owner was Richard Husbands who had letters of marque. In June 1652 Husbands placed the deponent in command of a captured Flemish sloop and gave him power to seize other ships in Virginia. He captured the <u>Fame</u> which was trading in Virginia and put a crew on board to bring her back to England but the Commissioners in Virginia summoned Husbands on shore and detained him there until he consented to surrender the <u>Fame</u> to them with an English merchant on board named <u>Giles.</u>

Thomas Muns of Ratcliffe, Middlesex, mariner aged 24. He served as gunner on the <u>Hopeful Adventure.</u>

Benjamin Cowell of St. James, Dukes Place, London, surgeon aged 26. He was surgeon of the <u>Hopeful Adventure</u> which seized the <u>Fame</u> under an Act of Parliament prohibiting foreigners from trading in Virginia but Richard Bennett's officers in that plantation claimed the ship.

John Allen of St. Gregory, London, gent aged 42. He was a passenger in the <u>Hopeful Adventure</u> which seized 2 Dutch vessels.

RE THE FORTUNE. 4 to 26 November 1652.

Thomas Pott of Bethnal Green, Stepney, Middlesex, mariner aged 29. In October 1651 he commanded the <u>John and Thomas</u> which carried goods and servants to

ENGLISH ADVENTURERS

Virginia to be delivered there to Daniel Benyon, son of Gabriel Benyon. Other goods and passengers belonging to the same merchants were carried in the John and Catherine commanded by John Miller. After Virginia had been reduced to obedience to the Commonwealth in March 1652, Daniel Benyon and Major John Carter, factors for Richard Glover, bartered the goods and servants for tobacco which they loaded on the Dutch ship, the Fortune, Mr. Cornelius Symons, since no space could be found on any English ship. The Fortune was then seized by the frigate Warwick, Captain Day.

John Horne also loaded many goods in the John and Thomas and took passage in her when she joined the fleet which was commanded to the West Indies to assist Sir George Ascough in the reduction of Barbados and Virginia. Horne, who had often ventured his life for the Parliament, also had to load his tobacco in the Fortune because the English ships returning from Virginia were already filled with tobacco obtained in exchange for the Scottish passengers they had carried outwards.

William Claiborne the elder, Deputy Governor and Secretary of Virginia, and John White also loaded tobacco on the Fortune. John White went from England to Virginia in 1650 while his brother William White went in the Margaret, Captain Arthur Bayly, in October 1651.

Daniel Benyon of St. Michael, Crooked Lane, London, merchant aged 24, son of Gabriel Benyon. He and Major John Carter loaded tobacco in Virginia in the Seven Sisters, Captain Abraham Read, which left Virginia with other ships of the English fleet in June 1652. The remainder of the tobacco consigned to Gabriel Benyon and Richard Glover in London was put aboard the Fortune when she arrived in James River and she was given leave by the Governor to carry it to England or Holland. Thomas Alexander also loaded tobacco on her. After she had been seized the Fortune was carried to Plymouth. John White had served the Parliament in many of their wars by land.

ENGLISH ADVENTURERS

George Holcroft of Redriffe, Surrey, mariner aged 45. He served on the John and Thomas and returned from Virginia in the Fortune which had loaded at Heart's Content at Lynn Haven in James River.

William White of St. Martin, Ludgate, London, citizen and woollen draper of London, aged 36. He sent goods to his brother John White in Virginia in October 1651.

John Horne of St. Matthew, Friday Street, London, citizen and salter of London, aged 34. He went to Virginia in the John and Thomas and returned in the Fortune. Of the claimants who went to Virginia with the fleet which sailed in October 1651, Nicholas Trott and George Holcroft are well affected to the Parliament. Thomas Alexander went to Virginia in the Honor.

Thomas Alexander of St. Michael, Wood Street, London, citizen and grocer of London, aged 22. Nicholas Trott went to Virginia in the Honor commanded by John Larramore, and George Holcroft in the frigate Ginney of which he was chief mate.

Richard Luckett of St. Swithin, Bush Lane, London, citizen and draper of London, aged 32. Nicholas Trott, whom he has known for 12 years, is well affected to the Parliament and has been in Commonwealth service.

John Rice of Wapping, Middlesex, surgeon aged 41. He was surgeon of the John and Thomas.

William Claiborne of Virginia, merchant aged 16, son of William Claiborne. When he was in Virginia he received goods which he bartered for tobacco on behalf of his father who had lived in Virginia for 31 years. The deponent came home in the Fortune.

Abraham Read of Ratcliffe, Middlesex, mariner aged 36. He was Captain of the Seven Sisters.

ENGLISH ADVENTURERS

VOLUME 67

RE THE WELCOME. 23 February 1652/3.

George Abbot of St. Michael Royal, London, merchant aged 35. He was merchant passenger on the Welcome, Mr. John Cutting, which loaded tobacco on account of the deponent and Richard Lapley in Virginia and left James River for London in May 1651. In June 1651 she was captured by a French man of war off the Scilly Isles and taken to Ushant in Brittany where she was confiscated.

----- WOODYE & ----- UPTON v. THOMAS GREENE.
12 March 1652/3,

Henry Wild of Dover, Kent, mariner aged 29. Thomas Greene hired Woodye and Upton to serve on the John and Sarah for a voyage to New England and Barbados. On her homeward voyage the ship was taken by a Dutch man of war.

Joane Greene, wife of Thomas Greene, of St. Olave, Southwark, Surrey, mariner, aged 25.

William Guy of St. Mary Magdalene, Southwark, Surrey, mariner aged 23. He served on the John and Sarah.

RE THE ADVENTURE OF NEW ENGLAND.
5 April 1652.

Henry Groome of Redriffe, Surrey, aged 48. He was Master's mate of the Adventure, Mr. Thomas Graves, which left Boston, New England, for London on 31 December 1651. On passage she was damaged by violent storms and had to be refitted before she arrived in London on 4 March 1651/2. There were 40 men in her company and she carried 80 passengers from New England who were safely delivered in London. Her owner was Francis Willoughby of New England.

ENGLISH ADVENTURERS

John Bristow of Wapping, Middlesex, ship carpenter aged 45. He served as carpenter on the <u>Adventure</u>.

James Heyden at present living in St. Dunstan in the East, London, planter in New England, aged 44. He served as steward on the <u>Adventure</u> which Francis Willoughby built for himself in New England.

FOR DAVID SULLICK, THOMAS KIMBOLD & PETER BUTLER. 17 August 1653.

Peter Butler of Boston, New England, mariner aged 37. David Sullick, Thomas Kimbold, Peter Butler, Captain Davenford, Mr. Allen, John Hardy and others of New England built the <u>Mayflower</u> in New England for their own use and appointed the deponent as her Master. In July 1652 she was hired to David Sullick, William Alford and the deponent for a voyage from New England to Virginia where she was to collect tobacco and return. On her homeward passage she was damaged by storms and lost her provisions and her company were obliged to eat raw hides for 20 days. On 27 December 1652 she was forced to put into Santo Domingo under a flag of truce and was seized there. For 4 days her company were inhumanly treated by the Spanish who gave them no food during that time after which they were relieved by the English there.

John Boreman of Ratcliffe, Middlesex, mariner aged 40. He was master gunner of the <u>Salvatrice</u> at Santo Domingo in Hispaniola when the <u>Mayflower</u> was obliged to take shelter there in a damaged condition. Her company were unable to move from their ship because they were so weak from lack of food.

VOLUME 68

JOHN PRICE v. WILLIAM SMITH.
3 to 6 December 1652

Thomas Dawes of Shadwell, Middlesex, where he has

lived for 5 years, aged 30. He was Master's mate of the 120 ton West India Merchant, of which John Price was Master and part owner, for a voyage from Southampton to Virginia in 1651 carrying goods and passengers. In October 1651 she was diverted to Barbados to attend to the English fleet because of which she did not arrive in Virginia until February 1651/2. There she loaded tobacco for Mr. Hussey, Mr. Pinhorne and other merchants of Southampton where she arrived in June 1652. William Smith had received payment for the freight of goods and passengers.

William Potts of Newcastle, Northumberland, where he has lived for 6 years, mariner aged 20. He is apprenticed to John Price with 6 months remaining to serve and was present when Price bought a one-eighth share in the West India Merchant. On her arrival back in Southampton in June 1652, Smith and 10 others came and seized the ship by violence.

John Chamberlayne of Southampton, apprentice to John Price, aged 17. He began his apprenticeship in 1651.

THOMAS REDBEARD v. GIFFORD BALE & EDWARD HOLCOMBE. 10 March 1653/4.

Thomas Robinson of Ratcliffe, Middlesex, mariner aged 35. He was gunner of the Report, Mr. Edward Dunning, a ship of 350 tons carrying 12 guns, which in January 1653/4 sailed for Virginia with 25 seamen and 12 passengers. Off the Isle of Wight she was sunk on 17 January by the frigate Ruby through the carelessness of her Captain, Edward Curtis.

Henry Gray of Redriffe, Surrey, mariner aged 21. He served on the Report.

VOLUME 69

ELIZABETH LONGSCROFT v. JAMES GARRETT.
20 February & 1 March 1653/4.

ENGLISH ADVENTURERS

Thomas Packer of St. Margaret Lothbury, London, mariner aged 27. James Makins deceased, to whom Elizabeth Longscroft is executrix, went as a common seaman on the New England Merchant, Mr. Carwithy, from London to Boston, New England, in May 1653. Carwithy died in Boston and was succeeded as Master by James Garrett. On the return voyage the ship was engaged by 2 Dutch men of war off the English coast in December 1653. Makins was wounded during the encounter and died 4 days later.

William Wood of Limehouse, Middlesex, mariner aged 46. He was gunner of the New England Merchant.

VOLUME 70

WILLIAM MORTON v. JOHN SPENCER.
5 to 8 September 1654.

Richard Lee of London, gent aged 34. He was at Jeremiah Harrison's plantation on Queen's Creek, York River, Virginia, in January 1653/4 with Harrison and William Morton (commonly called Sir William Morton) when Major Henry Norwood, Morton's factor, delivered tobacco aboard the James, Mr. Nathaniel Cook, in exchange for 3 servants and 3 dozen shoes.

William May of St. James Town (sic), Virginia, where he has lived for 4 years, but now residing in Fetter Lane, London, merchant aged 35. He went to Virginia in the Flower de Luce of London in 1650 together with 3 servants carried on Morton's account who were sold to Jeremiah Harrison. James Attersoll, a shoemaker in Virginia, made 3 dozen shoes and delivered them to Morton's factor in satisfaction of a debt and these were sold to Harrison for tobacco. A Mrs. Clarke was also indebted to Morton.

Thomas Forty of St. James Town, Virginia, where he has lived for 4 years, but now resident in Fetter Lane, London, planter aged 35. He went to Virginia with the deponent May when 3 servants belonging to Morton were shipped aboard at Gravesend. The defendant John Spencer is brother-in-law of Jeremiah Harrison.

FOR SAMUEL ANDREWES OF LONDON.
21 November 1654.

Phillip Cobbin of Plymouth, Devon, mariner aged 44. He was gunner of the Unity, Mr. Thomas Browne, of which the owners were Samuel Andrewes and Samuel Yeo of Charles Town, New England. In January 1653/4 iron hoops and other goods were loaded at Bilbao destined for the West Indies but, after she had sailed, the Unity was attacked and captured by the Sally man of war. The ship's company were taken on the Sally to Santa Cruz and 30 Moors were put aboard the Unity. Samuel Yeo is now resident in Bilbao.

William Morris of Charles Town, New England, carpenter aged 36. He was carpenter of the Unity.

JOHN DELL v. ROGER KILVERT. 29 January 1654/5.

Robert Herrington of Wapping, Middlesex, where he has lived for 20 years, but born at Southhold, Suffolk, mariner aged 36. He was boatswain of the John's Adventure when she was built 4 years ago in New England and became her gunner in 1652. She was owned by Roger Kilvert & Co. and her Master was Richard Thurstone. The ship made return voyages from London to New England in 1651 and 1652 and on each occasion the deponent collected provisions from John Dell now deceased.

RALPH WINGFIELD v. GEORGE & MATTHEW ABBOTT.
13 March 1654/5.

James Bonnell of Limehouse, Middlesex, mariner aged 21. He was purser of the Phoenix, Mr. Francis Steward, which loaded tobacco at Virginia in December 1653 on account of Ralph Wingfield and George Abbott.

Nathaniel Butcher of St. Mary le Bow, London, aged 23. In 1652 he was servant to Ralph Wingfield who despatched goods to Virginia on behalf of George Abbott in the Dolphin, Mr. Edward Gunnell, consigned to Matthew Abbott. Further goods were sent in November 1653 in the Phoenix.

SAMUEL WARNER v. RICHARD HOMER.
29 May 1655 to 30 January 1655/6.

Thomas Penryn of Garlick Hill, London, aged 21. As servant to Samuel Warner he went passenger in the Angel from London to Virginia on 31 October 1654. At Christmas time they met with violent winds which drove the ship into Barbados where she was condemned as a wreck after many of her goods were lost or damaged. Amongst the goods saved were 3 servants valued at £30 who were disposed of in Barbados while other salvaged goods were shipped from Barbados to Virginia in the Henry and David, Mr. Pensack.

Thomas Hastler of Crutched Friars, London, surgeon aged 25. He went in the Angel from London intending for Virginia on his own affairs.

Richard Homer of Ratcliffe, Middlesex, mariner aged 24. The Angel was a stout ship when she left London but was badly damaged in a storm on 21 December 1654 when she was 80 leagues from Virginia. A conference was called on board by Samuel Warner's factor when it was agreed that the voyage to Virginia should be given up and that the ship should proceed to Barbados. The Hopeful Luke which was bound to Virginia at the same time was cast away in the same storm.

JOHN JEFFERYS v. RICHARD HULL.
THE LORD PROTECTOR v. THE RAPPAHANNOCK ON AN ALLEGATION OF EDWARD GOODWIN.
15 June to 6 July 1655.

ENGLISH ADVENTURERS

John Shakerley of Falmouth, Cornwall, where he has lived most of his life, sailor aged 19. He served on the Rappahannock, Mr. Richard Hull, which was owned by John Jefferys, for a voyage from Cowes, Isle of Wight, to Virginia where she arrived last Michaelmas. On her return voyage with a loading of tobacco she was first seized by a Brest man of war and then retaken by a Commonwealth man of war. The Brest men threw overboard the letters being carried in the Rappahannock.

Richard Hull of Stepney, Middlesex, where he has lived for the past 16 years, but born at Lassick near Truro, Cornwall, mariner aged 35. He, John Jefferys of St. Clement's Lane, London, and Thomas Coleclough of Cornhill, London, were owners of the Rappahannock now in the River Thames. She left Gravesend on 12 September 1654 and arrived in Rappahannock River on 14 December. Having left there on 27 March 1655 she was seized near the Isle of Wight on 22 April but on 5 May 1655 retaken by a Commonwealth ship, the Hopeful, and a privateer, the Hound. The Rappahannock carried 9 iron guns and was a Dutch built ship captured from the Dutch in the late wars: she was bought by her present owners for £800 from Major Thompson.

GEORGE SWANLEY v. GEORGE JOHNSON.
16 July 1655 to 12 September 1656.

John Lee of Ratcliffe, Middlesex, mariner aged 26. He went boatswain of the Providence, Captain George Swanley, to Virginia where, in May 1654, George Johnson ordered tobacco to be loaded for his own account to be taken to London. After his departure from Virginia to New England, Johnson left the ship's merchant, David Sellick, to complete the loading. But Sellick died in Virginia and his widow broke open letters on the ship addressed to George Johnson in England in order to discover what quantities of tobacco had been shipped.

ENGLISH ADVENTURERS

George Johnson of Canterbury, Kent, merchant aged 27. When he was called away from Virginia to New England he entrusted his tobaccos to David Sellick and Stephen Horsey, his attorney in Virginia, by deed signed at Accomack on 22 May 1654 in the house of Nicholas Waddilow. The deponent had previously sent tobacco to London in the Thomas and Anne, Captain Fox.

Susanna Tilghman at present at St. Botolph without Bishopsgate, London, wife of Robert Tilghman of the same, merchant, aged 34. She was at Accomack, Virginia, with her late husband David Sellick when the Providence came there to collect tobacco to be freighted by her then husband. Nicholas Waddilow of Accomack had freighted tobacco in the Charles at £7 per ton. After her husband's death, George Swanley refused to sign Bills of Lading for any of Sellick's tobacco loaded on George Johnson's account. The deponent sent her servant aboard the Providence to ask for Sellick's letter to Johnson to be opened in order to ascertain to whom the various tobaccos were being consigned. (Vol. 71).

FOR THE EXECUTORS OF CAPTAIN JOHN WORDSWORTH. 13 October 1655.

Isaac Howe of Ratcliffe, Middlesex, mariner aged 30. He was Master's mate of the Hopeful Luke, Captain John Wordsworth, which left Gravesend for Virginia on 11 September 1654. She met with bad weather and was forced on to the rocks at Bermuda on 12 December 1654 where she broke up. Some of her cargo was brought ashore.

John Hawkins of Ratcliffe, Middlesex, surgeon aged 56. He went as surgeon of the Hopeful Luke. Goods salvaged from the ship were left in the hands of Thomas Richards, a merchant living in Bermuda.

TOBY SEVERNE, WILLIAM WOODS & RICHARD HUSBANDS v. ALEXANDER BENCE & WILLIAM ALLEN. 22 October 1655.

ENGLISH ADVENTURERS

William Flewen of Stepney, Middlesex, shipwright aged 40. He was carpenter of the Charles which was in Virginia at the same time as the Hopeful Adventure which sprang a bad leak after having loaded tobacco. He and William Davies, carpenter of the Hopeful Adventure, could not at first find the leak but eventually made repairs to enable the ship to return safely to London.

Thomas Bryan of St. Botolph, Aldgate, London, citizen and cooper of London aged 25. He was cooper of the Charles of London.

FOR JOHN THOMPSON & CO.
23 to 28 November 1655.

Robert Dillick of Shadwell, Middlesex, mariner aged 43. He was cooper of the Small Mallaga Merchant, owned by John Thompson & Co., which was pillaged by a French man of war while on a voyage from the West Indies to New England. Being left without provisions the ship's company were obliged to seek refuge at Santo Domingo under a flag of truce but the Spanish Governor seized the ship and imprisoned her men.

Peter Butler of London, mariner aged 38. In 1653 he went Master of the Mayflower of New England for a voyage from Virginia to New England but because of foul weather was obliged to put into Santo Domingo where he met Captain John Thompson. The deponent was also detained there for 6 or 7 weeks and came away with Thompson in a ship of Palma.

James Cowse of London, merchant aged 29. While he was at Palma in April 1653 a vessel named the Trinity arrived there carrying John Thompson and other Englishmen including Nathaniel Maverick who had also been held prisoner at Santo Domingo.

----- WINCHURST & ROGER YOUNG v. SAMUEL **ANDREWES.** 19 January 1655/6 to 18 August 1656.

ENGLISH ADVENTURERS

William Glanvile of Shadwell, Middlesex, mariner aged 24. He was Master's mate of the 156 ton Edward, Mr. Roger Young, which left London in September 1654 and arrived at Fyall on 23 October where she discharged goods on behalf of Samuel Andrewes. She took on board wines for New England and delivered them to Andrewes' factors at Boston. The ship then proceeded to Virginia where she arrived on 7 April 1655, loaded tobacco, and left on 12 June. She delivered her cargo in London on 23 August 1655.

William Allen of Billeter Lane, St. Catherine Creechurch, London, mariner aged 24. Captain Husbands was the commander of the Edward.

John Cliff of Tower Hill, mariner aged 53 (of All Hallows, Barking, London, aged 56 in August 1656). He was quartermaster of the Edward. (Vols. 70 & 71).

John Sauvaker of Stepney, Middlesex, mariner aged 27. He served on the Edward. When she arrived at New England Richard Russell, factor for Samuel Andrewes at Charlestown, came aboard with a cooper named Thomas Brigden to reassure himself that the wines were in a good state. (Vol. 71).

VOLUME 71

WILLIAM WILKINSON & CO. v. JAMES WAREING alias WARREN. 26 January to 3 March 1655/6.

Edward Alsop of St. Olave, Southwark, Surrey, mariner aged 30. He was Master's mate of the Exchange, of which William Wilkinson was Master and part owner, for a voyage with passengers and goods for Virginia in October 1654. She took on board a pilot, James Wareing alias Warren, to take her from the Thames to the Downs and he proved to be a factious man who often cursed the deponent and had said in his presence "a plague split this ship." She went on to the sands at Reculver, broke her rudder, and became incapable of continuing her voyage.

ENGLISH ADVENTURERS

John Humphrey of St. Mary Magdalene, Southwark, Surrey, mariner aged 32. He has been a mariner for 16 years and was boatswain of the Exchange which was of 240 tons and required at least 28 or 30 men to sail her, but only 22 were on board; 14 Englishmen, 1 boy, 2 Scotchmen and 5 Dutchmen. By repute Wareing was an able pilot.

Sidrach Wills of Ratcliffe, Middlesex, mariner aged 28. He was second mate of the Exchange.

FOR THE STATE. 10 March & 23 April 1656.

Captain Thomas Breedon of St. Peter, Paul's Wharf, London, brewer aged 36. He was at Salem, New England, in August 1653 when Captain Robert Harding and his company brought in a ship named the Spirito Santo which had been captured at Barbados with a cargo of hides and sugar. The prize was shared between Harding and his company and John Endicot, Governor of Massachussets, who bought the ship and renamed her the Happy Entrance.

William Brunning of Wapping, Middlesex, mariner aged 26. He was at Salem in August 1653 and was appointed by Thomas Breedon to be Master of the prize ship.

HENRY ASHURST, JACOB SHEAFE & CO. v. ROBERT HUBBART. 25 March to 1 April 1656.

Emanuel Springfield of Billericay, Essex, draper aged 21. In 1655 he came from New England to London as a passenger in the John's Adventure, Mr. John Cutting. During the voyage Cutting was in poor health, having hurt his head in a fall. The deponent can read and write and for as long as he attends the Court his board and lodging are paid by the plaintiffs.

Mary Springfield, wife of the above, aged 19. She has lived in New England from her birth until she left with her husband on the John's Adventure. She is able to read and can write a little.

Thomas Jenner of Charles Town, New England, mariner aged 28. He and Robert Hubbart sailed in the John's Adventure from Boston, New England, on 19 December 1655 bound for Nantasket and London. The Master's mate, Richard Browne, took aboard a consignment of beaver which he persuaded the boatswain, Gabriel Price, to assign to him. After the ship arrived in London John Cutting complained that the beaver was missing.

Thomas Glover of Aldermanbury, London, aged 29. He has known Jacob Sheafe of Boston, New England, and Henry Ashurst of London for 3 years. They traded together and the beaver had been loaded on their account.

John Cutting of Newberry, New England, mariner aged 63. He frequently transported goods belonging to Jacob Sheafe, whom he has known for 16 years, and who has traded with Henry Ashurst for 7 years. Because of the dispute which has arisen the deponent has been delayed in making his return voyage to New England.

Richard Browne of St. Olave, Southwark, Surrey, mariner aged 25. He was Master's mate of the John's Adventure and has known Jacob Sheafe for 4 years.

ARMIGER WARNER v. ALEXANDER HOWE & WILLIAM WATSON. 7 May 1656 to 12 November 1658.

Jacob van Zoiden of Cowes, Isle of Wight, surgeon aged 21. William Watson was Master of the Alexander from October 1652 to 10 August 1654 and in February 1653/4 sailed her from Ireland to York River, Virginia, where she arrived in May 1654. In the following August she left with a lading of tobacco.

Captain John Miller of Ratcliffe, Middlesex, mariner aged 44. He has been a trader in tobacco and other Virginia commodities for 8 years and Master of a ship bringing tobacco from Virginia. He was in Virginia when the Alexander was loaded and arrived home a week after her. At the request of Armiger Warner he had viewed her lading of tobacco. For the past 40 years 4 hogsheads of Virginia tobacco have been reckoned as a ton.

George Swanley of Bromley by Bow, London, mariner aged 39. He was Master of the Providence and was in Virginia at the same time as the Alexander. Other ships also there which left after the Alexander were the Cleere Anne of London and the Beaver of Bristol.

George Faulkener (Faulconer) of London, (of Deptford, Kent) merchant aged 40. (2 depositions). He used to live in Crooked Lane and other places in London but for 5 or 6 years has resided at Deptford. He has only a small estate, having suffered great losses at sea, but is only a very little in debt. He has traded to Virginia for 15 years and has made 3 voyages there. After the first voyage 16 years ago he stayed in Virginia for a year. His second voyage there was as supercargo of the Alexander which was owned by John Marston and chartered by Armiger Warner for a voyage from Falmouth to Cork and from there to Virginia and London. Since that voyage the ship has again been to Virginia for which her Master was Alexander Howe. The deponent's last voyage to Virginia was in the Expedition. (Vols. 71 & 72).

John Prynn of Newington Butts, Surrey, mariner aged 27. He was sent by John Marston to Cork to deliver a letter to William Watson about the voyage to Virginia.

John White of London, merchant aged 41. When the Alexander returned from Virginia he and Alexander Howe were employed as arbitrators in the dispute between Marston and Warner.

Captain Thomas Taylor of Wapping, Middlesex, shipwright aged 56. He had trimmed the Alexander, a ship of 300 tons. Virginia hogsheads are far greater than others and as big as English butts. (Vol. 72).

ENGLISH ADVENTURERS

William Wood of Wapping, Middlesex, merchant aged 49. He is part owner of the Alexander. (Vol. 72).

Simon Messinger of Shadwell, Middlesex, cooper aged 40. A ton occupies rather less space in a ship's hold than 3 Virginia hogsheads. (Vol. 72).

John Goodman of St. Catherine Coleman, London, cooper aged 34. He is a master cooper. (Vol. 72).

James Jauncy of St. Lawrence Jewry, London, citizen and grocer of London aged 34. He has been in the Virginia trade as an apprentice and freeman for 17 years and has dealt for 9 years in Virginia tobaccos of which he has received many hundred hogsheads. (Vol. 72).

Matthew Travis of St. John the Evangelist, London, citizen and salter of London aged 50. He has dealt in Virginia tobaccos for 30 years. (Vol. 72).

Richard Atkinson of St. Michael, Crooked Lane, London, citizen and embroiderer of London aged 30. For 15 years he has been a dealer in tobacco which he makes up and cuts. (Vol. 72).

PHILIP EWERS v. WILLIAM WATTS. 24 May 1656 to 14 February 1656/7.

Stephen Bonner of Redriffe, Surrey, mariner aged 30. He was Master's mate of the William, Mr. Philip Ewers, which sailed from Gravesend on 12 December 1654 to James River, Virginia, where she arrived on 22 April 1655 and loaded tobacco for William Watts whose factor in Virginia was Samuel Mathews Esq. When he went to collect tobacco from Robert Bourne he found that it had already been delivered, on Mathews' orders, to the Peter and John of London. Because of this the William was delayed in Virginia until 1 August 1655 and came home with a light lading. Amongst seamen it was accounted that the voyage from Gravesend to James River took 3 months, sometimes more and sometimes less. The William made only one port on her outward voyage, at Falmouth where she was driven by the adversity of the weather.

Francis Canter of Wapping, Middlesex, mariner aged 32. He was gunner of the William and has made 2 voyages to Virginia in her. She is a ship of 200 tons. He has made the voyage to Virginia in 8 weeks but at other times it can take 3 or 4 months.

John Harris of St. Mary at Hill, London, merchant aged 36. He has been a Virginia merchant for 15 years.

John Jefferys of St. Clement Eastcheap, London, merchant aged 40. (2 depositions). He has been a Virginia merchant for several years. The William was entered at Gravesend as being bound for Barbados. Because the rates demanded for freightage of tobacco by that ship were too high he arranged for shipment of his tobacco by the Providence of London, Captain Swanley. Virginia tobacco which remained uncollected by English ships after March had to be bartered away against payment in the following year or sent to New England. If kept in Virginia after March it became spoiled by the heat.

William Wilkinson of Shadwell, Middlesex, mariner aged 56. He was employed by Philip Ewers to pilot his ship from the Thames to the Downs. Ewers and his wife came aboard her at Tilbury but left at Lee where Ewers' wife had kinsfolk. The deponent sent word to Ewers through his brother-in-law Mr. Bonner when the ship was ready to sail but received no reply, and when Ewers finally returned there was argument about which channel they should take. The deponent finally brought the William to anchor in the Downs in January 1655/6 and left her.

James Jenkins of Gracechurch, Fenchurch Street, London, merchant aged 56. He was part owner of the Seven Sisters, Mr. Abraham Read, which cleared Gravesend in November 1654 and arrived in Virginia in February 1654/5. Had the William reached Virginia in time he would have freighted tobacco on her but instead used the Charles of London.

Laurence Thompson of Ratcliffe, Middlesex, mariner aged 37. He went passenger and carried freight in the William to Virginia and returned home in her. There were such long delays in the outward passage that it was said in Virginia that the ship was cast away or taken by the French.

Edward Gunnell of Ratcliffe, Middlesex, mariner aged 50. He has traded for Virginia tobacco for 15 years and has made 11 or more voyages there. He went as Cape merchant to Virginia in the Peter and John which sailed with the William from Gravesend. When they left the Downs they were in company with the Recovery, Mr. John Younge. The Peter and John arrived in Virginia on 22 April 1655 and Ewers' ship a few days later.

John Fitch, citizen and merchant of London aged 25. He went passenger to Virginia in the William and left her at James River. He stayed in Virginia for 18 months afterwards.

Richard Bennett, born at Wilscombe, Somerset, an inhabitant of Virginia but at present living in London, Esq aged 49. He has been an inhabitant of Virginia for 28 or 29 years, is a merchant for tobacco, and was Governor in 1654/5 when the William arrived in Virginia. The first ships to arrive in that year at the end of January or beginning of February were the James, the Golden Lion, the Seven Sisters and the John and Katherine. The Margaret, Mr. Robert Fox, arrived shortly before Ewers' ship and Ewers confessed to the deponent that he had been delayed by difficulties over manning and piloting.

Thomas Potter of London, merchant aged 39. He has traded in Virginia tobacco for 15 years. In October 1654 he was at the Downs in the Crescent, Mr. Thorowgood, in company with the James of London, the Golden Lion, the Seven Sisters, the John and Katherine and several other ships which all arrived in Virginia in January or February and returned without dead freight. In the same year the deponent , Arthur Bayly and Mr. Kent shipped tobacco from Virginia in the Margaret, Mr. Robert Fox, which was driven into Antigua by adverse weather and, because she was delayed there for repairs, did not arrive in Virginia until April 1655 and thereby lost much of her lading. In the subsequent dispute between himself and Bayly, who owned the Margaret, the arbitrators appointed were Mr. Jolliff, William Allen, John Jefferies and Captain John Miller, all merchants of London.

Tobacco will not keep in Virginia from one harvest to the next because of the heat and after mid March the inhabitants give up any expectation of sending tobacco to England by English ships and use any vessels they can. They also send tobacco to New England.

Captain John Whitty of All Hallows, Barking, London, mariner aged 36. He went to Virginia as Master of the Freeman of London and on 25 November 1654 was at Gravesend with the William but departed before her. The Freeman arrived in James River, Virginia, with the Seven Sisters on 26 January 1654/5 and remained there until 30 May 1655.

THOMAS ALLEN, ANTHONY PENISTON & CO. v. JOHN WRIGHT, JASPER WHITE, PERIENT TROTT, THOMAS TOMLINSON, JOHN BUTTS, RICHARD CHANDLER & GEORGE WATERMAN. 11 June 1656.

William Welch of Shadwell, Middlesex, shipwright aged 22. He was carpenter of the King of Poland, Mr. Frederick Johnson, which was owned by the plaintiffs. In June 1655 she loaded tobacco at Bermuda and went on to Nansemum, Virginia, to load more to be delivered to the defendants. On 27 January 1655/6 she left James River bound for London but ran into a tempest on 1 February and was damaged. She arrived in London on 22 March 1655/6.

Jonathan Pooke of Ratcliffe, Middlesex, mariner aged 28. He was gunner of the King of Poland.

Thomas Vicar of Ratcliffe, Middlesex, but born at Gothenburg, Sweden, mariner aged 23. He was a common seaman on the ship.

Josiah Elfreth of Wapping, Middlesex, mariner aged 37. He was chief mate.

William Pethebridge of Ratcliffe, Middlesex, mariner aged 45. He was a mate.

WILLIAM BROWNING & CO. v. WILLIAM BULKLEY.
21 June 1656 to 3 February 1658/9.

Jacob Baker of Wapping, Middlesex, mariner aged 21. He was carpenter of the Plain Dealing of which William Browning was the Master and part owner. On 28 May 1655 she cleared Gravesend loaded with goods belonging to William Bulkley, John Pratt and Anthony Wills and, after her arrival in New England on 25 August 1655, delivered them to Bulkley's factor, John Jolliff. The ship then loaded pipe staves and tobacco, leaving on 18 September 1655 for Faro in Portugal. At Faro William Browning sought the opinion of the Captains of other English ships whether it was safe, because of the hostilities between England and Spain, to go on to Malaga for which the Plain Dealing was intended. Learning that it was not he unloaded his cargo at Faro and took aboard figs, almonds, oils and other commodities to be delivered to London. While on passage there the ship was surprised on 19 February 1655/6 by an Ostend man of war and taken as a prize to Ostend.

Thomas Bordfield of Shadwell, Middlesex, mariner aged 32. He was a passenger on the Princes of London, Mr. William Osgodby, which was seized in Malaga on 31 August 1655 with another English ship, the Anne and Joyce, Captain Piles, but the latter contrived to escape by cutting her cables.

Thomas Bargrave of Wapping, Middlesex, mariner aged 36. He was Master of the Friendship which in October 1655 was chased at sea by 2 French men of war and, to avoid capture, she put in to Lisbon. There he was advised that it was unsafe for him to trade to any Spanish port and therefore went to Faro where he saw the Plain Dealing.

Thomas Baudes of London, merchant aged 30. During 1655 he resided in Spain and until March 1656/7 was an English factor at Malaga. Trade with English merchants was embargoed from 10 September 1655 until March 1656/7 although English ships were permitted to unload at Malaga, and Captain Browning might also have been able to do so.

Richard Pendarves of London, merchant aged 24. In 1655 he was resident in Malaga and received notice from his partner Robert Hubbold, a London merchant, to expect the Plain Dealing from New England. (Vol. 72).

James Boord of Deal, Kent, mariner aged 35. He went as mate and boatswain of the Plain Dealing. (Vol. 72).

WILLIAM BULKLEY v. EDWARD MILBERRY.
27 to 28 January 1656/7.

Richard Riggs of Southampton, mariner aged 29. He went as mate of the Southampton Merchant, Mr. Edward Milberry, for a voyage from Salem, New England, in August 1654, to Dover or London. At that time she was a good, stout ship owned by William Bulkley of London, merchant. On passage she encountered bad weather, was broken open and, being unable to continue her voyage, put into Southampton. Her cargo of hides was found to be badly damaged and was shipped to France.

Esaiah Gardner of Southampton, mariner aged 33. He was Master of the vessel which took the hides to France after they had dried out at Southampton.

Edward Milberry of Southampton, mariner aged 33. He was Master of the Southampton Merchant.

SAMUEL EDWARDS & ROGER WHITFIELD v. SAMUEL BUSHELL. 9 March 1656/7 to 1 May 1657.

George Byrnes of Dublin, Ireland, surgeon aged 19. He has been to sea for 29 months in the negro trade and before that was in State service in the Primrose. He was surgeon of the Negro, Mr. John Lockier, which in 1655 went from Ireland to St. Christopher's and returned to London by way of Jamaica, New England and Madeira. Her gunner, Samuel Edwards, and her carpenter, Roger Whitfield, were often distempered and drunk during the voyage and insubordinate to the Captain. After discharging negroes at St. Christopher's in June 1655, Lockier discovered that one of his shirts was missing and the deponent found it to be in the possession of one of the planter's servants. He noticed this especially because the women there are used to have nothing on their arms but their under garments. The shirt had been given her by the ship's steward, Thomas Wetherall, who frequented her house.

James Carter of Limehouse, Middlesex, mariner aged 23. He shipped on the Negro in New England in June 1656. She loaded corn and pipe staves there for Madeira but much of the corn was damaged because of the inadequacy of the bulkheads. When the ship arrived at Southampton Samuel Edwards was accused of stealing wine from her stores.

Thomas Wetherall of Ratcliffe, Middlesex, aged 59. He has served as a seaman and steward for 6 years. John Everett and Benjamin Beare of the Negro stole a small anchor from the ship in New England but alleged they had found it in Jamaica. The merchants and owners of the ship were Alexander Howe and Robert Rich. She arrived in London in February 1656/7.

John Lockier of Limehouse, Middlesex, mariner aged 35. He has been a seaman for 17 years and a Master for 10.

ENGLISH ADVENTURERS

Thomas Morgan of Redriffe, Surrey, mariner aged 34. He was boatswain of the Negro and believes Edwards and Whitfield to be honest, sober men. (Vol. 72).

Thomas Gowen of Disert, Scotland, mariner aged 30. He joined the ship in New England in June 1656 and also believes the plaintiffs to be honest and sober. (Vol. 72).

Henry Man of Enchusen, Holland, mariner aged 31. He was carpenter's mate of the ship which he joined at St. Christopher's in April 1655 and left at Boston, New England, on 1 May 1656. (Vol. 72).

Roger Worthley of ?Noell, Norfolk, mariner aged 45. He was gunner's mate of the Negro which he joined in New England after several of her company had deserted. But for the help of the plaintiffs the ship could hardly have got back to England. (Vol. 72).

FROM COUNTRY EXAMINATIONS BUNDLE 264

FOR WALTER JAGO, GEORGE KENNYCOTT, JOHN HAYNE AND JOHN HOYLE, OWNERS OF THE SWALLOW OF DARTMOUTH.
Dartmouth, 25 May 1657.

Hugh Reynolds of Kingswear, Devon, mariner aged 33. Thomas Horsman went as Master of the Swallow on 17 December 1652 for a voyage from Dartmouth to Virginia by way of Nevis.

Richard Carew of Dartmouth, surgeon aged 43. He went as ship's surgeon.

Thomas Lewis of Dartmouth, joiner aged 64. The owners ordered the ship to Nevis to be refitted.

Andrew Stocker of Kingswear, Devon, mariner aged 37. When the Swallow was in Plymouth 6 years ago he and Joseph Baker of Plymouth, merchant, sold her to her present owners.

ENGLISH ADVENTURERS

Edward Lidston of Stoke Fleming, Devon, shipwright aged 40. He went on the <u>Swallow</u> as carpenter's mate.

Nicholas Cruse of Dartmouth, Devon, shipwright aged 44. He worked on the <u>Swallow</u> as chief carpenter for 4 months before she sailed. (HCA13/264).

RE THE RECOVERY OF BRISTOL.
Bristol, 15 October to 2 November 1657.

George Proctor of Bristol, where he has lived for 16 years, mariner aged 40. In 1655 Nicholas Tilly, Henry Dighton and Alexander Gray, owners of the <u>Recovery</u>, freighted her to Samuel Norris and Nicholas Holwey, merchants of Bristol, for a voyage to New England under James Smith as Master. She sailed from Bristol on 20 September 1655 with cloth, shot, lead, etc. which she discharged in Portugal in October. The deponent served only 3 months on this voyage but has heard that James Smith took his ship to Ireland on her homeward passage and that she was arrested at his suit.

John Jones of Bristol, where he was born and bred, mariner aged 55, deposes about the wages paid to James Smith.

Arthur Hollester of Bristol, gent aged 33. He has always dwelt in Bristol and formerly used the trade of clerk but is now Under Chamberlain of Bristol. The ship's owners reached an agreement with James Smith in the Swan Tavern, Bristol.

James Smith. Oils were loaded on his ship in Portugal which she unloaded at Barbados in February 1655/6. She then went to New England where in May 1656 she loaded goods for a return voyage to Barbados where she arrived in July 1656. On her return voyage to Ireland, she met with violent storms in December 1656 which stripped her rigging and did not arrive at Kingsale until 4 January 1656/7. (HCA13/264).

JOHN JEFFERYS & ROBERT LLEWELLYN v. JACOB MOULSON, ----- SMITH & -----FRANKLYN.
19 to 23 November 1657.

Robert Oldfield of Spalding, Lincolnshire, gent aged 22. He went passenger in the Unity, Mr. Jacob Moulson, which sailed from Gravesend in June 1654, in order to reside in Maryland in Virginia with Mr. Cornwallis. The ship was detained in the Downs by contrary winds until August 1654 when she went to Dublin. There White, a factor for the plaintiffs, had promised to provide a full loading of servants but only 30 could be found though others were obtained by Jacob Moulson. After loading, 2 servants escaped in the ship's skiff and another, a woman who was suspected of being a witch, was put ashore by the general consent of the passengers and crew because they feared she would be dangerous to the voyage.

The Unity sailed from Dublin in September 1654 but was detained at Courtrai, France, by contrary winds and then encountered a tempest before meeting the Matthew of London, Mr. Fox, and the Hopeful Luke at sea. They met with further storms in November and December during which the ship was holed but she was able to continue her voyage while the passengers manned the pumps continuously. Under threat from the passengers Moulson agreed to steer the ship for Barbados but missed his course and arrived at Antigua in January 1654/5 where the ship was viewed and declared unfit to continue her voyage. Before the Unity's passengers were disposed of the deponent went to Nevis and St. Christopher's where he heard that the Hopeful Luke had been cast away at Bermuda.

Samuel Church of Writtle, Essex, mariner aged 26. He was a private mariner on the Unity. The plaintiffs had agreed with the defendants, who were owners of the ship, to pay Jacob Moulson for the transportation of 200 servants from Ireland to Virginia but the ship was delayed in Dublin because of the small number available. It was reported in Dublin that the witch put aboard the <u>Unity</u> had been turned off another vessel bound for Virginia or Barbados. Moulson laid out his own money to procure a further 39 passengers but only 53 were put aboard in Ireland. After the ship had arrived in Antigua 2 servants escaped in a canoe while 13 died there and the deponent helped to bury them. 35 were sold at the best rates obtainable. The ship, which carried 24 mariners, remained for 18 months at Antigua awaiting repairs but these were never carried out.

Abraham Clarke of Deptford, Kent, shipwright aged 25. He was carpenter of the <u>Unity</u>. In Dublin Jacob Moule employed a local joiner to help procure 53 men and women to be shipped aboard as servants for Virginia. The witch who had been shipped prophesied that the <u>Unity</u> would never get away from Dublin while there was a whole block in her and, as soon as they had weighed anchor, the main Jew block, though strongly bound with iron, broke in pieces causing the mainyard to fall down. The witch also prophesied that the ship would not reach Virginia or Barbados and would suffer great extremities before reaching land without loss of life. The deponent took a woman servant aboard whom he sold at Antigua for 550 lbs of sugar.

CATHERINE KILVERT v. THE PROVIDENCE. 8 April 1658.

Hezekiah Usher of Boston, New England, stationer aged 42, testifies as to proceedings in Boston where a verdict was given for Colonel Temple on behalf of Roger Kilvert.

JOSEPH DREW & ROBERT GIBBS v. THE ADVENTURE. 17 May 1658.

Stephen Talby of Boston, New England, mariner aged 40. He was Master of the <u>Adventure</u> which left Boston on 18 December 1657 with a lading of sugar, oils, fish and skins. While she was between Plymouth and Dartmouth on 28 January 1657/8 she was captured by an Ostend man of war but, in an attempt to take her into Ostend, the Adventure ran aground on the coast of Normandy during a storm and was lost.

Daniel Williams of Horsey Down, Surrey, mariner aged 40. He was Master's mate of the Adventure. The Ostend man of war was commanded by a Scotsman named Hambleton.

Richard Croft of All Hallows, Bread Street, London, ironmonger aged 25. He had met Joseph Drew, Thomas Deane and Robert Gibbs to negotiate payment of their claims.

Edward Hicks, apprentice of the above, aged 22.

THOMAS MIDDLETON v. SIMON MESSINGER.
19 October 1658.

Thomas Mather of Shadwell, Middlesex, mariner aged 27. In May 1656 he went as purser of the Two Sisters, Mr. Henry Thompson, of which the owners were Simon Messinger, Robert Hooker, Samuel Hill, Thomas Thompson, William Thompson, John Gre-----, Peter Crumpton, Edward Thompson and Henry Reynolds, for a voyage to New England and Barbados. On 10 December 1656, a week before the ship arrived in Jamaica, Henry Thompson died and Philip Gorrell, the Master's mate, succeeded him. There were 28 mariners in the ship's company. In New England Nathaniel Silvester, factor for the plaintiff Colonel Thomas Middleton, and Peter Silvester loaded pease and pipe staves to be freighted to Barbados; and in Barbados sugar was taken on board but had to be discharged at Fyall after the ship had encountered bad weather which holed her. She was broken up in December 1657.

ELIZABETH SUTTON v. JOHN TULLY.
7 to 10 December 1658.

William Tooke of Wapping, Middlesex, mariner aged 30. He served on the Amity, Mr. John Tully, for a voyage to Virginia in 1654. William Sutton served with him but, being ill on passage, was allowed to go ashore at Virginia to recover his health at the house of the deponent's father, William Tooke. As Sutton was preparing to take the boat to return to his ship he collapsed on the deck and died. The deponent received all his goods and traded them for tobacco which he consigned to Elizabeth Sutton, the widow of the deceased.

Hester Tooke, wife of the above deponent, aged 29. In June 1654 the Amity discharged the tobacco which her husband had loaded at Virginia on behalf of Elizabeth Sutton but the latter refused to come for it. The deponent's husband had remained in Virginia.

FROM COUNTRY EXAMINATIONS BUNDLE 265

THE LORD PROTECTOR v. JOHN WHITE, NEHEMIAH BOURNE & CO.
Helston, Cornwall, 30 November to 1 December 1658.

Moyses Butler, merchant aged 25. He was factor of the White Rock of London, Mr. Solomon Clarke, which sailed from there in December 1657 with State provisions intended for Barbados and Jamaica. The ship went from Barbados to New England to load masts etc. and 2 chests of money at Piscataway and departed for London on 22 July 1658. On 22 August she met with 2 Spanish ships which she fought for 5 or 6 hours before being lost and driven ashore in Cornwall. Her owners were Nehemiah Bourne, John White, William Wood, Henry Roch and Solomon Clarke.

Richard Mitchell of Plymouth, Devon, shipwright aged 35. He joined the White Rock off Madeira as her carpenter to replace the former carpenter who had died.

The following deponents testify as to the disposal of

ENGLISH ADVENTURERS

salvage from the White Rock:

Peter Major of Fowey, Cornwall, merchant aged 29.

Oliver Chesworth of The Mount, Cornwall, Customs Officer aged 24.

John Eva of Penzance, Cornwall, cordwainer aged 30.

William Keigwin of Mousehole, Cornwall, gent aged 30.

Nicholas Boson of Newland, Cornwall, gent aged 34.

David Grosse of Marazion, Cornwall, sailor aged 40.

John Coppithorne of Penzance, Cornwall, gent aged 35.

John Tremaneice of Penzance, Cornwall, gent aged 35.

Peter Ceely of St. Ives, Cornwall, Esq aged 40.

Nicholas Warde of Cambourne, Cornwall, husbandman aged 35.

John Beare of Penzance, Cornwall, gent aged 31.

Henry Munday of Penzance, Cornwall, saddler aged 30.

John Richard the elder of Keivenhall near Lamorna Cove, Cornwall, yeoman aged 55.

John Richard the younger of the same.

William Boddenna the younger of Paul, Cornwall, aged 21. (HCA134/265).

VOLUME 73

THE LORD PROTECTOR v. ADRIAN TENNINCK.
2 to 11 April 1659.

Allen Allenson of Enchusen, Holland, but native of Dover, Kent, mariner aged 40. He was steersman of the <u>Jager</u> or <u>Huntsman</u> of Amsterdam which was at St. Sebastian in August 1658 when a Holland vessel, the <u>White Angel</u>, loaded with Virginia tobacco and bearskins, was brought there as a prize.

Thomas Pollard of Madenblick, Holland, mariner aged 33. The <u>White Angel</u>, Mr. Jacob Lawrenson, was loaded at Virginia in June 1658 with 340 hogsheads of tobacco and 200 bearskins by Henry Meese as factor for John Benbow and Thomas Cornwallis, subjects of the Commonwealth. On 6 July 1658 the ship was taken by a St. Sebastian frigate under the command of Captain Peter Chivers and her cargo was transferred to the <u>Crown and Sceptre</u> of Amsterdam, Mr. Jacob Hendricks Benning, by order of Mr. Adrian Tenninck, a Hamburger, to be taken to Amsterdam. The deponent was at Plymouth in March 1659 when he met the Master of the <u>St. Jacob</u> of Hamburg who confessed that he was carrying to Hamburg the tobacco and bearskins taken from the <u>White Angel</u> but had been forced into Plymouth by bad weather.

Henry Meese of London, merchant aged 30. He was in Maryland in April 1658 and there loaded goods on behalf of John Benbow and Thomas Cornwallis. He first met Benbow in London and has known him for 4 years, and first met Cornwallis in Maryland and has known him for 7 years. They are members of a company which includes John Harris of London, merchant, Samuel Tilman of London, mariner, and John ?Woode of Maryland, planter.

Maryland and Virginia are commonly spoken of under the name of Virginia alone, being contiguous places under the English and parted only by a river. Virginia is the more ancient discovery and the more considerable place.

Abdias Claesons Voghel of Amsterdam, mariner aged 31. He was Master of a vessel taken as a prize into St. Sebastian where he saw the <u>White Angel</u> being unloaded.

----- **CORSELLIS v. HENRY WARCUP.**
9 to 12 April 1659.

ENGLISH ADVENTURERS

In August 1658 the Golden Star, Mr. Thomas Sprettiman, was let to freight in Cadiz to Anthony Upton, factor for Christopher Boone of London, merchant, to carry wine from the Canaries to London. On passage she was seized by the Alexander, Captain Henry Warcup. Deponents in this case include:

John Frost of New England, mariner aged 22. He served on the Golden Star but is now one of the company of the Exchange of London, Mr. John Peirce.

John Clarke of New England, mariner aged 19, deposes similarly.

Thomas Sprettiman, native of Peterhead, Scotland, aged 37.

FOR CHARLES REEVES OF LONDON, MERCHANT. 20 May 1659.

Robert Gibbs of Boston, New England, mariner aged 25. In February 1657/8 the Gift of London, Mr. Samuel Scarlet, left London for Madeira and encountered foul weather on passage. At Madeira she was declared unfit for sea but nevertheless proceeded to Boston where she was judged a wreck. The deponent was Charles Reeves' correspondent in Boston.

Richard Price of Boston, New England, merchant aged 23. He has known Samuel Scarlet for 6 years.

RE THE SHEPPERD. 1 September 1659.

By Bill of Sale of 26 July 1659 signed in Amsterdam, Abraham Johnson sold to William Whittington, Lieutenant-Colonel William Kendall and John Micheel of Virginia a ship called the Christina Regina but now known as the Shepperd of Northampton. The following deponents testified in this case:

ENGLISH ADVENTURERS

William Whittington of Ackamack, Virginia, merchant aged 40.

William Melling of Ackamack, Virginia, merchant aged 49.

James Cade of the City of London, merchant aged 52.

FROM COUNTRY EXAMINATIONS BUNDLE 266

JOHN TRELAWNY & JOHN KINGE v. NICHOLAS OPYE. Plymouth, 4 to 26 April 1660.

In 1658 John Trelawny and John Kinge owned the 60 ton Orion of Plymouth, Mr. Leonard Randell, which was freighted by Nicholas Opye for a voyage to New England, Leghorne and to return to Plymouth. She sailed on 12 May 1658 and upon her arrival in New England was ordered to Newfoundland to load fish. From there she went to Barbados where her Master left a protest that her lading of fish in Newfoundland had been insufficient. At Barbados the Orion loaded sugar but was seized by the Spaniards on her homeward voyage. The deponents included:

John Webbe of Plymouth, mariner aged 29.

John Deringe of Plymouth, shipwright aged 30. He went as carpenter of the Orion which was consigned from New England to Francis Martyn and Thomas Jackson in Newfoundland who were Masters of 2 ships belonging to Nicholas Opye.

Francis Martyn of Plymouth, mariner aged 28.

Edward Wrisland of Plymouth, sailor aged 24.

James Hull of Plymouth, merchant aged 27. Francis Martyn was commander of the Delight and Thomas Jackson of the Supply, both of Plymouth. Nicholas Opye ordered Abraham Browne in New England to

-170-

load provisions on the Orion to be delivered at Newfoundland to Roger Coke and John Fosse, planters.

VOLUME 73 (continued)

Entry made 21 June 1660: **The King retourned, whom God long preserve.** Signed by Doctor Zouch, Judge.

RE THE HOPEWELL. 2 July to 27 September 1660.

William Jackson, servant of Thomas Burton of London, merchant, aged 21. John Jeffreys, James Jenkins, Thomas Coleclough, Thomas Burton and Richard Netmaker were owners of the Hopewell, Mr. Arthur Perkins, and freighted her in December 1657 for a voyage from London to Angola and Virginia. She was seized off the coast of Africa.

Humphrey Whyles of Wapping, Middlesex, mariner aged 33. In April 1659 he landed negroes in Virginia from his ship the Violet and not one was sold under £35 sterling.

William Woolrich of St. Clement Eastcheap, London, grocer aged 26. (In another deposition described as "aromatarius" - ?scent maker). He was purser of the Violet. The negroes they took aboard at Calabar are not generally considered as good as those of Angola.

FRANCIS WHEELER v. ----- PERYN.
25 July to 3 August 1660.

Thomas Beale of York, Virginia, planter aged 50. He lived near and well knew Francis Wheeler the elder who died at Christmas 1659 and his wife Elinor who died in April 1660.

Richard Evans of Wapping, Middlesex, cooper aged 40. He was cooper of the Honor, Mr. Robert Clemes, which loaded tobacco at York River for Francis Wheeler the elder. While he was in Virginia the deponent asked

Wheeler who should have his tobaccos if he died and was told: "Who dost thou think should have them but my child Franck for all my care is for him." Francis Wheeler the elder had made a will before departing for Virginia and Elinor Wheeler was mother-in-law to Francis Wheeler the younger in London.

Robert Clemes of Wapping, Middlesex, aged 37. He was Master of the Honor and, while he was in Virginia, Nicholas Trott of York Town, merchant, delivered to him a letter from Elinor Wheeler, written shortly after her husband's death, asking for his Bills of Lading to be handed to Trott.

Christopher Eveling of Ratcliffe, Middlesex, mariner aged 36. He was Master of the Thomas and Anne which also carried tobacco home for Francis Wheeler the elder.

Thomas Andrews of Ratcliffe, Middlesex, mariner aged 44. He was steward and quartermaster of the Thomas and Anne and met Elinor Wheeler at a funeral in Virginia a month after her husband had died. She then told him that her husband had left only one will which he had deposited with his son in England before leaving for Virginia.

Thomas Foster of St. Botolph, Aldgate, London, sailor aged 35. He was boatswain's mate of the Thomas and Anne.

John Ireland of Wapping, Middlesex, sailor aged 31. He was boatswain of the Thomas and Anne. Francis Wheeler the elder had cattle and other goods in Virginia.

JOHN HARRIS & JOSEPH BEOMONT v THE FORTUNE. 2 & 28 August 1660.

John Basford of St. Stephen, Coleman Street, London, tobacconist aged 42. He was employed by John Harris and Joseph Beomont to view and appraise tobacco at

St. Mary at Hill, London.

Thomas Griffin of St. Dunstan in the East, London, distiller aged 47. In September 1657 he viewed and appraised tobacco brought to London on the account of Harris, Beomont and a Virginia planter.

ARTHUR SPRY v. JOHN SPARROW, RICHARD BLACKWALL & HUMPHREY BLAKE.
13 August to 4 September 1660.

Elizabeth Webb, wife of Thomas Webb of Ratcliffe, Middlesex, aged 34. She was formerly wife of John Thompson who was Master of the Gift of God of New England from 1647 to 1650. The ship was owned by Arthur Spry. John Holle bought her in France in 1647 and her former husband sailed her from there to New England. In 1650 the ship was seized at Barbados by Sir George Ascough.

Elizabeth Wager, wife of Francis Wager of St. Martin in the Fields, Middlesex, aged 48. In 1654 she went to see John Thompson and his wife who told her about the Gift of God.

John Rowe of London, merchant aged 50. While he was in the City of London in September 1640 he received a letter from Arthur Spry in Plymouth asking him to insure the Gift of God which was then in Bilbao.

Renatus Enys of the City of London, merchant aged 31. In 1646/7 he was servant to Gregory Alford, an Englsih merchant living in Nantes, who told him he had sold the Gift of God to Arthur Spry. The deponent has known Spry, who was born in Cornwall, for 14 years.

ENGLISH ADVENTURERS

INTERROGATORIES 1609 - 1625

RE THE NEPTUNE. Interrogatories to be administered to Andrew Dixon (Dickeson).

The New England Company hired Andrew Dixon to build them a ship called the Neptune and to bring it from Whitby to London. Sir Ferdinando Gorges, Captain Edward Giles and Clement Swillman paid the workmen's wages and Thomas Scooler stood surety for Dixon. Through Dixon's carelessness the ship ran on to the rocks while on her way to London and had to be got off by Luke Fox and the ship's pilot, Giles Wiggener. (HCA 23/6/105).

RE THE EXCHANGE'S PRIZE. Interrogatories to be administered to Richard Laurence of Plymouth and to Humphrey Randoll.

The Exchange of London, Mr. John Blake, seized a pirate ship in the Bay of Consumption, Newfoundland, which was brought back to London by Humphrey Randoll. At the time of her capture the Phoenix of Plymouth was in Newfoundland. (HCA 23/6/293-295).

HILDEBRAND PRUSON v. DON DIEGO SERMENTO, LEGATE OF SPAIN.

James Muton, Nicholas Norborowe, Benjamin White and Daniel Hefry became bound to Hildebrand Pruson and Abraham de Baker to sail to the West Indies in the Peregrine, the Grissell and the Hopewell to cut wood there and to discover an island called Green Island or, if they failed, to go to Virginia and trade for goods there. The ships were taken and robbed by the Spaniards. (HCA 23/6/494).

WILLIAM RAND v. DON DIEGO SARMIENTO, LEGATE OF SPAIN.

ENGLISH ADVENTURERS

The <u>Little John</u> of Sandwich, Kent, Mr. William Rand, went to the West Indies to cut wood, which it had been the practice of English ships for some years to do. While in the islands of Hispaniola many negroes came voluntarily aboard to be freed from the savages who had killed some of their number. The savages in those parts unsually kill negro children as soon as they are born lest they should increase, and also devour any Spaniards they capture.

William Taverner late of Plymouth, Devon, mariner. In 1606 he shipped in the Greyhound of Amsterdam for a merchant voyage to the West Indies but the ship sprang a leak and was forced into the Streights for repairs. When she put into Tunis she was seized by the Turks who put her company on shore. The deponent was there for 3 months for want of a ship home but then took passage in the Unicorn of Bristol to the Southern Cape and from there took a Plymouth ship to Galicia. 24 November 1609.

John Paine late of Plymouth, Devon, sailor. He engaged for the same voyage with William Longcastell, William Taverner, Samuel Cade and other Englishmen to the number of 15. 28 November 1609.

John Elliott of Sumford, Devon, sailor. In 1608 he engaged for a voyage to Trinidad and Guam in the Wilmott of Topsham, Mr. Robert Holland, which was owned by Lewis Plumley. The ship sprang a leak and was obliged to sail to Mogador in Barbary where she was cast away. 9 June 1610.

Thomas Ford of Tower Wharf, London, sailor aged 34. He served on the Archangel of London, Mr. William Little, for a voyage to Trinidad for tobacco. Andrew Miller went as ship's merchant and there was bad will between him and the Master. Once Miller drew his dagger at Little on board and challenged him to a fight. From Trinidad the Archangel sailed to Hispaniola where the deponent and 4 others went ashore in a pinnace to trade with the negroes but, finding none, began to cut down a palm tree to bring back on board. As they did so 13 Spaniards and negroes came suddenly out of the woods and set upon William Little and a negro struck him with a lance, causing him to fall as though dead. The rest of the party hid in the bushes until night when they made their way back to their ship and sailed for England. 25 October 1611.

William Wright of Dartmouth, Devon, mariner aged 30. In April 1610 he was engaged by Alexander Shapley of Kingswear, Master of the Restitution of Dartmouth, to go as trumpeter on a fishing voyage to Newfoundland in his ship. While she was on her return passage to Portugal she was seized on 20 September 1610 by Captain Robert Stephens and his company and taken on board a ship laden with nails which had been captured by Captain William Smith. On the same day Captain Stephens took 2 other ships coming from Newfoundland, the Delight of Topsham and a vessel from Barnstaple. Captain Stephens and Captain Smith kept company with another pirate called Captain Drinkwater, a Fleming, who commanded a flyboat of 140 tons, etc. etc.
14 December 1611.

Edmund Towers of the City of London, merchant aged 24. He was factor for John Davis who in April 1611 loaded iron, silks and linen aboard the Abigall, Mr. William Mills, for a trading voyage to Guinea and the West Indies. The ship was taken at sea by Captain Peter Pecke and Captain John in 2 Holland men of war. Pecke took some of the goods captured from the Abigall to Amsterdam. 17 June 1612.

Thomas Glasier of the City of London, servant of John Davis (above), aged 22, deposes similarly.
17 June 1612.

Jeffrey Slater of London, surgeon aged 25, examined on an allegation brought by the Spanish Ambassador. In January 1611/12 Captain Hughes of the Raven seized a Portuguese ship and brought her cargo of sugar to London. Tobacco brought to London in the Raven was first seized at Marmora by Peter Pecke in his Flemish man of war from a Spanish ship coming from the West Indies. 20 June 1612.

ENGLISH ADVENTURERS

Anthony Smith of Limson near Exeter, Devon, ship carpenter aged 30. He served in the Raven. Captains Stephens, Baugh, Smith, Hughes and Franck seized the Spanish West Indies ship from Peter Pecke.
20 June 1612.

Robert Jenkins of Cardiff, sailor aged 21. He also served on the Raven. 20 June 1612.

James Paine of Yarmouth, mariner aged 30. He was hired by Sir Thomas Smith in May 1611 to go to Virginia with Sir Thomas Gates and there to engage in a fishing voyage with James Gentleman, Mr. John Simpson, Edward Pr(enderg)ast, Gottard Thurtells, Robert England, William Lawson, Edward Turner, ----- Hubberdyne and a boy. They set out fishing in May 1612 in the Discovery belonging to the Virginia Company but the weather was foul and thick and they told the Master of the vessel that they would not come any more to Virginia and wished to return to England. They therefore sailed to Dartmouth and Dover from where the deponent came to London carrying a letter to Sir Thomas Smith from the ship's Master. They brought nothing from Virginia but a little salt and met only with a ship of Colchester coming from the Islands and with a French ship from which they obtained bread.
2 July 1612.

Morris Jones of London, surgeon aged 25. In December 1611 the Daisy of London, Mr. John Buntinge, set out from London on a merchanting voyage to the West Indies. Robert Tindall went in the ship which was taken by pirates while at Guinea in January 1611/12 etc. etc. 24 October 1612.

VOLUME 48

James Burges of Ratcliffe, Middlesex, mariner aged 50. In 1613 his son, Thomas Burges, who was apprenticed to Richard Scott, sailmaker of Ratcliffe, was hired to go

as sailmaker on the Resistance of London, Mr. Edmond Clifton, for a merchanting voyage to the West Indies. John Price was hired as Master's mate. The ship went to the West Country where she took on board Captain Mannering. After the ship had been at sea for some months allegedly on course for the West Indies, Mannering altered course and took to plundering.
17 November 1614.

Thomas Wisdom of London, barber surgeon aged 30. He went as surgeon of the Resistance. To his distress and that of Burges and Price, Mannering went among the pirates. 17 November 1614.

Edward Willmouth of Millbrooke, Cornwall, mariner. He was Master of the Willing Mind of Foy which went on a fishing voyage to Newfoundland. In August 1614 4 ships of war under Captain Mainwaring (Mannering) came aboard her and took her victuals and sent her crew on shore. There the crew ran into the woods to hide in order to escape joining the pirates, and some made their way home in the Edward and John of Foy. 5 April 1615.

Thomas Tucker of Newcastle, mariner. In October 1611 he shipped as Master's mate on the Daisy of Sandwich, Mr. John Buntinge, for a voyage to the West Indies. On passage she was seized by Captain Easton of the Conrad who took out the deponent and others from their ship and detained her for 3 months before she could proceed on her voyage. Easton had 5 other ships under his command, the Valentin, the Jacob, the Swan and 2 prizes. 22 July 1615.

Robert Walsingham of London, mariner, deposes similarly. The Daisy was seized off the coast of Guinea. 16 July 1618.

Nicholas Thompson of Ratcliffe, Middlesex, sailor. In 1614 he shipped in the Hopewell of London, Mr. John Powell, for a voyage to the West Indies, but was left ashore at Plymouth from where he shipped in the James of ?Topsham, Mr. Thomas Neeson, for Venice. The James was taken by pirates near Portugal, etc. etc. 14 December 1615.

Humfrey Randall of Salcombe, mariner aged 34. He was Master of the Hope of London belonging to Mr. Humfrey Slany and others of the Newfoundland Company. In November 1615, while she was homeward bound with a loading of fish, she was seized off Dover by a pirate ship commanded by Lawrence Mountaine and owned by Mr. Hawkins of Harwich. 22 December 1615.

John Crofoote of Salcombe, sailor aged 18. He has been to sea for 2 years under Mr. Humfrey Randall and served in the Hope during her fishing voyage to Virginia. 6 March 1615/16.

Richard Anlobye of Rippon, Yorkshire, sailor. He came from the West Indies with Sir Warham St. Leger in the Thunder to St. Ives, Cornwall. The deponent was left ashore when the ship left St. Ives etc. etc. 3 July 1618.

Nicholas Scott of Hull, sailor, deposes similarly. 3 July 1618.

Richard Foxe of Hull, mariner, deposes similarly. 11 July 1618.

William Douglas of Wapping, mariner. He was Master of the Gilliflower of London and in September 1618 was in Newfoundland when one of his company, William Branham of Horsey Down, was taken by pirates and is still detained by them. 21 January 1618/19.

Edward Exton of Southampton, merchant aged 32. His factor at Newfoundland, Edward Guy, wrote to him on

17 August 1619 to inform him that he had loaded fish on the Collett of Southampton to be shipped on the deponent's account to Bordeaux. Since the ship was never heard of again she must be presumed lost. 6 April 1620.

Jacob Breme of Lambeth, merchant. In March 1618/19 the pinnace Silver Falcon of Dover, Captain John Fenner and Master Henry Bacon, sailed from Dover with a cargo worth £900 for Bermuda, Virginia and the River of Canida to trade, plant and discover. Her crew were hired by one Andrewes who died before the voyage was undertaken, and Lord Zouch and his adventurers appointed Captain Fenner. After 4 or 5 months the Silver Falcon returned to Holland and unloaded more than 20,000 weight of tobacco which had been trucked with a West Indies frigate off Bermuda. Starchye was Master's mate of the Silver Falcon and James Wood the gunner's mate. 13 May 1620.

Richard Stafford of Staplehurst, Kent, gent aged 25, examined on an allegation of the Spanish Ambassador. Daniel Elfrith, whom he has known for 5 years, went as Master of the Treasurer in 1619 to the West Indies where he was in company with a Dutch ship. When the Treasurer brought into the Somer Islands 25 negroes the then Governor, Captain Kendall, suspected that they had been taken at sea from a Spanish ship and caused them to be put into a longhouse at St. George's Town. Some were then sold and others hired out by Captain Butler, now Governor. The Treasurer left the Somer Islands in February 1619/20. 3 June 1620.

John Weston of Oxford, gent aged 22. He has known Daniel Elfrith for 18 months. The Treasurer arrived in the Somer Islands in September 1619 bringing a small amount of tallow and grain. 3 June 1620.

Hugh Wentworth of Basingstoke, Hants, yeoman aged 28. He has known Daniel Elfrith for 18 months. When the deponent left Bermuda the Treasurer lay moored at

ENGLISH ADVENTURERS

St. George's Town. 3 June 1620.

Reinold Booth of Reigate, Surrey, gent aged 26. He has known Daniel Elfrith for 10 years. In 1619 the deponent went on the Treasurer from Virginia to Bermuda and at the end of June 1619 she was compelled, while in the West Indies, to consort with a Flemish man of war, the White Lion of Flushing, commanded by Captain Chope who threatened to shoot at the Treasurer unless Elfrith complied with his wishes. Chope had permission to seize Spanish ships and in mid July 1619 he took 25 men from his own and Elfrith's ships and sailed away in a pinnace. After 3 days he brought back a Spanish frigate which he had captured and, out of goodwill towards Elfrith, gave him some tallow and grain from her. Immediately after this the deponent left the Treasurer in the Seaflower for Bermuda and departed from there for England. 23 July 1620. (See also **WARWICK v. BREWSTER** p. 12ff).

VOLUME 49

Thomas Schowler of Wapping, Middlesex, anchorsmith aged 44. Andrew Dixon, whom he has known for 4 years, came to him in Wapping to commission the making of anchors for a ship being built in Whitby for the New England Company. The deponent went to Whitby and joined Dixon and a party of carpenters which went into the woods there to hew timber for the construction of the keel. 16 June 1624.

Christopher Davies of Ratcliffe, Middlesex, shipwright aged 24. He worked on the ship at Whitby and came in her to London when she was finished. On passage up the River Thames she fouled one of the King's ships at Deptford. 17 June 1624.

William Mills of St. Botolph, Aldgate, London, carver aged 33. He did the carving work on the ship. 17 June 1624. (See interrogatories on p. 174).

ENGLISH ADVENTURERS

Thomas Hamon of Limehouse, Middlesex, sailor aged 25. In 1624 he went as boatswain of the Unity, Mr. Tobias White, for a voyage to Virginia, Canada or New England. The ship was owned by Henry Beale and Peter Leonard who freighted her to Humphrey Rastell and ----- Griffith. She left the Thames on 9 April 1624 and took up a course for Virginia but, since the year was far spent, Rastell changed the orders and directed White to sail for New England where she arrived on 24 June. There she made ready to carry her passengers on to Virginia but Rastell then embarked them on another vessel on which he sailed himself. Three months after his departure the Unity was ready to leave New England for London but Captain Wolverstone received orders from Rastell that she was to proceed instead to Virginia. On 21 November 1624 the Unity sailed on a course for Virginia with 6 passengers from New England and collected bread and provisions from Mountheginge Island. She then encountered contrary winds for most of a month, at the end of which all hope of reaching Virginia was abandoned and course was set for England. She arrived back in Blackwall at the end of February 1624/5.
11 May 1625.

VOLUME 50

William Cleybourne of Virginia, Esq. He has had dealings in Virginia for many years. He sent Lieutenant Ratcliffe Warren in a little boat armed with a gun into Maryland to demand the return of a pinnace and goods which the Marylanders had taken from him. He does not remember the occasion perfectly but recalls that he signed a letter for Warren to take with him. The inhabitants of the Isle of Kent suffered extreme want because their pinnaces and goods were taken from them by the Marylanders and persuaded the deponent to give them leave to recover them. Lieutenant Warren returned to the Isle of Kent with a boat which the deponent gave into the custody of the Governor of Maryland.
16 April 1638.

NAME INDEX

Abbott, George 141,145,
      146
Abbott, Matthew 145,146
Abbott, Richard 119
Adams, Robert 131
Agborowe, Francis 50
Agener, Nicholas 52
Ahuddus, Conrade Noteman
      40
Alderton, ----- 26
Aldridge, Augustine 66,
      77,78
Aldridge, Martin 66
Alexander, Thomas 139,
      140
Alford, Gregory 173
Alford, William 142
Alkin, Sampson 59
Allen, ----- 110,142
Allen, James 24
Allen, John 31,32,35,138
Allen, Philip 127
Allen, Thomas 157
Allen, William 111,131,
      148,150,157
Allenson, Allen 167
Allerton, Isaac 16
Alsop, Edward 150
Altham, Emanuel 16
Anderson, Robert 54,55,
      68,107,114
Andrewes, ----- 101,181
Andrewes, Peter 19,24,
      41,45-52
Andrewes, Samuel 145,149
      150
Andrews, Thomas 172
Andrewes, William 126
Anlobye, Richard 180
Anthony, ----- 107
Anthony, William 66,67
Argall, Sir Samuel 12,
      13,14

Arlabeer, Edward 121,122
Armitage, Robert 72
Arnold, John 24
Ashbye, Thomas 93
Ashcroft, John 57
Ashton, Thomas 82
Ashurst, Henry 151,152
Askewe, Thomas 52
Atherall, Richard 71
Atkins, Richard 23
Atkinson, Raphe 31
Atkinson, Richard 154
Atterbury, William 106
Attersoll, James 144
Atye, Charles 38
Audley, Thomas 103
Austen, Anthony 101
Austen, Edward 29
Austin, ----- 132
Austrey, James 95,96
Ayscough, Sir George
      139,173
Ayscough, John 103

Babb, John 31
Babb, Thomas 63,64
Backenhurst, John 95
Bacon, Henry 16,181
Baker, Jacob 158
Bayly, Arthur 139,157
Bailye, Robert 20
Baker, Ambrose 34
Baker, Andrew 103
Baker, James 22
Baker, John 30
Baker, Joseph 161
Baker, Thomas 103
Baldwin, Henry 18
Baldwin, John 121
Bale, Gifford 143
Bally, John 33,34
Baltimore, Lord 64,65,
      104,105

NAME INDEX

Bamstone/Bemstone, Roger 114,115
Banckes, Jacob 16
Banckes, William 27
Banister, Alexander 23
Barbone, Praise 59
Bardwell, John 121,124
Bargrave, Thomas 159
Barker, Edmund 15
Barker, George 96
Barker, John 74
Barker, Robert 99
Barker, William 23,82
Barkley - see Berkeley
Barnard, Richard 40
Barnes, Edward 70
Barnes, Henry 109
Barnes, Richard 29
Barnes, Thomas 29
Barrett, Humphrey 26
Barrett, Thomas 29
Barton, Samuel 109
Barum, Anthony 89
Barwicke, Christopher 93
Basford, John 172
Basill, John 78
Baskerfield, ----- 58
Bassocke, Edward 11
Bateman, Edward 72,98
Bateman, William 87
Bateson, Matthew 21
Batson, Richard 100,106, 107,131,132
Baudes, Thomas 159
Baugh, Capt 178
Baxter, Roger 102
Baxter, Stephen 127
Bayly - see Baily
Baynes, ----- 109
Beadle, William 48
Beale, Edward 23
Beale, Henry 107,183
Beale, John 60,61,107

Beale, Thomas 63,171
Beomont, Joseph 172,173
Beamont, Richard 13
Beane, ----- 44
Beare, Benjamin 160
Beare, John 167
Beaton, Richard 109
Beckett, Thomas 96
Beddell, Daniel 21
Bell, ----- 48
Bell, John 76
Bell, Thomas 125
Bell, William 90
Belson, John
Bemstone - see Bamstone
Benbow, John 168
Bence, Alexander 148
Bendlowe, Richard 67
Benger, William 122
Bennett, Edward 12,54
Bennett, John 77
Bennett, Richard 54,73, 74,133,138,156
Benning, Jacob Hendricks 168
Bennington, Richard 108
Bensly, James 54
Bentley, ----- 64
Benyon, Daniel 139
Benyon, Gabriel 139
Beomont - see Beamont
Berkeley, William 35
Barkley, William 45
Besbech, Thomas 75
Besse, William 07
Best, ----- 121,122
Best, James 83
Bettant, ----- 86
Betts, Leonard 98
Bevan, Roland 126
Bidle, Daniel 21
Bigge, John 75
Biles, Robert 32

-185-

NAME INDEX

NAME INDEX

NAME INDEX

NAME INDEX

Gardiner, Edward 7
Gardiner, Henry 28
Gardner, Arnold 11
Gardner, Daniel 126
Gardner, Esaiah 159
Gardner, Samuel 137
Garland, Thomas 111
Garner, Thomas 123
Garnet, William 129
Garnetot, Peter 36
Garretson, Martyn 40
Garrett, James 143,144
Gates, ----- 11,12
Gates, Sir Thomas 104,
                    178
Gauntlett, William 11
Gaurney, Francis 55
Gawden, Francis 19,20
Gayne, William 11
Geantott, Peter 35
Gear, Robert 17
Gentleman, James 178
Gibbons, Edward 115,128
                    129
Gibbs, John 37,54,127,
                    128
Gibbs, Jonathan 116
Gibbs, Robert 164,165,
                    169
Gilbert, Rawleigh 2
Giles, ----- 138
Giles, Abraham 83
Giles, Edward 174
Giles, William 97
Gill, William 135
Gillam, Benjamin 44
Gillam, William 58
Gilmett, Thomas 88
Glanvill, ----- 97
Glanvile, William 150
Glascocke, John 87
Glasier, Thomas 177
Glover, Richard 139

Glover, Thomas 152
Godfrey, Nicholas 55
Godfrey, William 87
Godney, Edward 105
Golde, Rowland 11
Goodman, John 154
Goodwin, Edward 146
Gorges, Sir Ferdinando
                 3,26,174
Gorrell, Philip 165
Gorton, Stephen 92,94,95
Gough, Jeffrey 58
Gowen, Thomas 161
Grace, George 76,84
Grafton, Joseph 126
Grant, John 66,67
Graves, Adam 122
Graves, Matthew 48,51,
                    112
Graves, Thomas 141
Gray, Alexander 162
Gray, Henry 143
Greene, ----- 117
Greene, Charles 67
Greene, Joane 141
Greene, Thomas 141
Greene, William 24,62,
                   63,78
Greete, Malachy 33
Gretwood, John 58
Greve, Hugh 28
Gribble, Richard 72
Griffin, Thomas 173
Griffin, William 47
Grigge, Francis 39
Grimes, Gilbert 97
Grinder, Thomas 101
Grister, John 72
Groome, Henry 141
Grosse, David 167
Grove, Anthony 9
Grove, Richard 42
Groves, Adam 121

NAME INDEX

NAME INDEX

Hutchins, John 111
Hutchinson, Henry 73,74
Hutchinson, William 73,
             74,75
Hutton, David 86
Hutton, Gilbert 93
Hynd, Robert 27

Ibbutson, Henry 13
Ingle, Richard 85,94,
             104,110
Ingleton, William 135
Ireland, John 172
Irish, John 116
Ivatt, John 95

Jackson, ----- 111,115
Jackson, James 57
Jackson, Lewis 113
Jackson, Margery 57
Jackson, Thomas 170
Jackson, William 171
Jacobs, Thomas 35
Jacobson, Nicholas 68
Jago, Walter 161
Jake, John 130
James, ----- 101
James, Jonas 78
Jancey, ----- 121
Jauncey, ----- 132
Jauncy, James 154
Jansen, Matthias Johnson
             134
Jasperson, John 133
Jeanes, William 95
Jefferys, John 146,147
          155,157,163,171
Jeffreys, Roger 119
Jeffryes, Nathaniel 14
Jenkins, Capt 30
Jenkins, James 155,171

Jenkins, John 55
Jenkins, Robert 178
Jenkins, Walter 58,59
Jenks, ----- 109
Jenner, Thomas 152
Jennings, Richard 124
Jesson, Nathaniel 133
Jobson, John 75
John, Capt. 177
Johns, John 98,99
Johns, Richard 48
Johns, Robert 99
Johnson, ----- 78,131
Johnson, Abraham 169
Johnson, Andrew 72,109
Johnson, Francis 28
Johnson, Frederick 116
                157
Johnson, George 147,148
Johnson, Henry 58
Johnson, James 36
Johnson, John 7,40,111
Jolliff, ----- 157
Jolliff, John 158
Jollye, Nicholas 75
Jones, Anthony 73,74
Jones, Daniel 31,51
Jones, John 23,162
Jones, Morris 178
Jones, Robert 120
Jones, Thomas 11
Jones, William 67,68,117
Jordan, Joseph 87
Jourdaine, Elias 131
Jourdaine, Samuel 119
Jucie, John 116

Keigwin, William 167
Kemble, Thomas 128
Kempton, Richard 65
Kendall, Capt. 181
Kendall, William 169

NAME INDEX

NAME INDEX

NAME INDEX

NAME INDEX

Ships

Elizabeth & Mary 107
Elizabeth & Sarah 86
Elizabeth Bonadventure
      29
Endeavour 36
Exchange 150,151,169
      174
Expedition 42,43,47,
      153
Faith 28,52,53
Falcon 11,30,31,107
Fame 138
Flower de Luce 76-86
     106,144
Freeman 157
Friendship 25,26,159
Garland 6-11
George 8,29,48,49,51,
      105
Gift 169
Gift of God 2,3,22,23,
      173
Gilliflower 7,180
Ginney 140
Golden Dolphin 135
Golden Lion 133-137,
      156
Golden Star 169
Grace 22
Greyhound 176
Grissell 174
Happy Entrance 151
Henry 50,51
Henry & David 146
Honor 140,171,172
Hope 67-69,105,114,180
Hopeful Adventure 138
      149
Hopeful Luke 146-148,
      163
Hopewell 23,63,64,171,
     174,179

Ships

Hound 147
Hunter 27,28
Huntsman 168
Increase 53,54,124,125
Jacob 179
Jager 168
James 15,144,156,180
Jane 27,108
Jane Bonadventure 22
Jarvas 29
Jason 108
John & Barbara 73,74
John & Catherine 139,
      156
John & Dorothy 60-62
John & Isaac 116
John & Sarah 141
John & Thomas 137-140
John Goodfellow 102
John's Adventure 145,
     151,152
Jonas 32,33
Jonathan 11,17,18
Jonathan & Abigail
   121,122,123,124
Joseph 39
King of Poland 157,158
Lion's Whelp 37,38
Little Anne 63
Little James 16,17
Little John 175
Little Neptune 70,71
London Merchant 22
Lyon 35,36
Marathon 16
Margaret 139,156,157
Marmaduke 18
Mary 114,115,125,126,
      131
Mary & John 2
Mary Constance 109,110
Mary Fortune 44,45

NAME INDEX

NAME INDEX

Ships

Thomas & Anne 148,172
Thomas Bonadventure 52
Thunder 180
Treasurer 12-14,181,
    182
Trinity 149
Tristram & Jane 77,87,
    88
Truelove 55,80,92-95
Two Sisters 165
Ulysses 1
Unicorn 41,176
Unity 111,112,145,163,
    164,183
Valentin 179
Vintage 25
Violet 171
Virginia Merchant 120
Warwick 6,7,10,12,26,
    139
Welcome 141
West India Merchant
    134,135,143
Whale 29
White Angel 168
White Lion 182
White Rock 166
William 23,24,29,40,
    101,126,154-157
William & George 117,
    121
William & John 133,
    135,136,137
William & Ralph 120,
    132
William & Sarah 110
Willing Mind 179
Wilmott 176

Shotton, Mary 131
Shuckborowe, William 127
Shute, Richard 106

Siddall, Alice 4
Siddall, William 4,5
Silver, Thomas 98
Silvester, Nathaniel 165
Silvester, Peter 165
Simons/Symons, Stephen
    37
Simpson, John 178
Singleton, Edward 18
Sisson, Giles 123
Sixtye, ----- 107
Skinner, John 120,132
Skinner, William 53
Slany, Humfrey 180
Slater, Anthony 76
Slater, Jeffrey 177
Small, John 111
Smallwood, Humphrey 124
Smallwood, Matthew 41
Smith, ----- 100,101,163
Smith, Anthony 178
Smith, Edward 11
Smith, Francis 30,69,70,
    91,95,96
Smith, George 05
Smith, Giles 18
Smith, James 162
Smith, John 9,26,57,58,
    86,110,118,119
Smith, Matthew 97
Smith, Nicholas 133,134
Smith, Roger 89,122
Smith, Samuel 103
Smith, Sir Thomas 178
Smith, Thomas 14,29,35,
    53,86,118
Smith, Tobias 108
Smith, William 77,79,82,
    83,85,142,143,177,178
Snowe, ----- 114
Soame, Edward 15
South, Robert 39
Southwood, John 87

Spackman, Nicholas 74
Sparrow, John 173
Spencer, John 144,145
Spencer, William 89
Spicer, Capt. 115
Spinkard, ----- 109
Sprettiman, Thomas 169
Springfield, Emanuel 151
Springfield, Mary 151
Spry, Arthur 173
Spurgin, George 120
Stafford, ----- 84
Stafford, Benedict 112
Stafford, Richard 181
Stafford, William 77
Stagg, ----- 54,114,115
Stagge, Christopher 34
Stagge, Thomas 72,98,
104,135
Stanton, Thomas 120
Stapleton, George 126
Starbucke, William 60
Starchye, ----- 181
Starchye, Richard 42,43
Starky, Henry 16
Starr, John 22
Staveley, John 136
Steede, William 109
Steele, Laurence 119
Steele, William 81
Sterne, Bartholomew 67
Stevens, John 108
Stephens, Philip 120
Stevens, Philip 132
Stephens, Richard 24
Stephens, Robert 177,178
Stevens, William 16,17,
70
Stevenson, ----- 85
Stevenson, William 131
Steward, Augustine 13
Steward, Francis 145
Stircke, George 20

Stocker, Andrew 161
Stone, James 73
Stone, John 118
Stoner, John 54
Stratford, Henry 27
Strawe, Nicholas 79,81
Strelley, Patrick 100
Stringer, John 77
Studd, Erasmus 64
Sturges, ----- 107
Sturman, John 102
Sturman, Thomas 102
Sullick, David 142
Surgo, Michael 1
Surtis, Richard 107
Sutcole, John 124
Sutcole, William 124
Sutton, Elizabeth 165,
166
Sutton, William 166
Swanly, ----- 108
Swanley, George 147,148,
153,155
Swanton, Capt. 30
Sweet, ----- 22
Swillman, Clement 174
Symons, Cornelius 139

Talbot, Peter 90,109
Talbot, William 131
Talby, Stephen 164
Tamage, ----- 82
Taply, George 33
Tappan, John 71
Tasker, Edward 70
Tatton, Henry 76
Taverner, Henry 49,50,
51,86
Taverner, William 176
Tawny, Henry 14,15
Tayler, ----- 109
Taylor, George 58

Tayler, John 43,44
Tayler, Philip 109
Taylor, Richard 27
Taylor, Thomas 61,130,
         153
Tayler, William 77,79
Temple, Col. 164
Tenninck, Adrian 167
Thierry, James 66
Thierry, John 56-58,66,
        67,80,83
Thomas, Peter 25
Thomas, William 115,126,
        131
Thompson, Major 147
Thompson, Edward 36,37,
        165
Thompson, George 42
Thompson, Henry 165
Thompson, John 149,173
Thompson, Lawrence 137,
        156
Thompson, Maurice 12,29,
    31,39,42,55,76,96,
    98,103,107,111,112
Thompson, Nicholas 179
Thompson, Stephen 66
Thompson, Thomas 165
Thompson, William 165
Thorowgood, ----- 156
Thoroughgood, Capt. 84
Throgmorton, Thomas 108
Thurmer, John 135
Thurstone, Roger 145
Thurtells, Gottard 178
Tibbetts, Henry 20
Tickner, William 41
Tilghman, Robert 148
Tilghman, Susanna 148
Tilley, John 122
Tilly, Nicholas 162
Tilman, Samuel 168
Tilson, Thomas 106,110

Tindall, Robert 178
Todd, Thomas 31
Tokelye, Robert 60
Tomlinson, Thomas 157
Tooke, Hester 166
Tooke, William 166
Towers, Edmund 177
Tranchmore, Robert 78
Tranchmore, Thomas 77
Transcombe, William 71
Travis, Matthew 154
Trelawny, John 170
Trelawney, Robert 114
Tremaneice, John 167
Trevise, Nicholas 43,44,
        128
Trevore, William 40
Trewergy, Nicholas 127
Trimingham, John 21
Trott, Henry 121,124
Trott, Nicholas 140,172
Trott, Perient 157
True, John 37
Trundle, Robert 123
Tucker, Lewis 45,62
Tucker, Richard 138
Tucker, Thomas 179
Tucker, William 11,22,43
Tully, John 165,166
Turgess, Simon 106
Turley, Francis 132
Turner, Edmond 86,87
Turner, Edward 178
Turner, John 119,130
Turner, William 81
Turtle, Robert 102,105
Twine, Marles 32
Twisell, Henry 121
Twisse, Nicholas 128

Ubancke, Henry 102
Ulye, Mrs. 90

NAME INDEX

Upton, ----- 141
Upton, Anthony 169
Usher, Hezekiah 164

Vane, Lord 67
van Heusden, Lawrence
117
van Remont, John 40
van Zoiden, Jacob 152
Varvell, Thomas 124,125
Vassall, Samuel 19,24,
45,46,48-51,55,56
Vaughan, John 115
Vega, ----- 15
Velasco, Alphonso de 2
Vennard, Abigail 67,68
Vennard, Christopher 67,
69
Venner, Thomas 59
Verdon, Jonas 5
Vertrill, Walter 40
Vicar, Thomas 158
Vines, ----- 26
Violett, John 77
Virginia Co 5,8-10,178
Voghel, Abdias Claesons
168

Waddilow, Nicholas 148
Wadham, Thomas 32
Wadmer, John 130
Wager, Elizabeth 173
Wager, Francis 173
Waimouth, Titus 138
Wake, Richard 107
Walker, ----- 47
Walker, John 103
Walsingham, Robert 179
Walters, John 25
Waltham, John 11
Walton, Henry 85

Wannerton, Thomas 39
Warcup, Henry 168,169
Warde, Nicholas 167
Warde, Pliney 34
Wareing, James 150,151
Warner, Armiger 152,153
Warner, Samuel 146
Warner, Thomas 68
Warner, William 3,4
Warren, James 150,151
Warren, Ratcliffe 183
Warren, Robert 77,78
Warren, William 96
Warwick, Robert Earl of
12-14
Wasbury, ----- 114
Waterman, George 157
Waters, John 92
Waters, Margaret 92
Watlington, Isaac 70,92,
93,95
Watson, ----- 64
Watson, John 116
Watson, William 152,153
Watts, William 154
Wayborne, John 29
Weale, ----- 60
Weatherley, Capt. 26,27
Witherly, Thomas 30,33
Webb, Elizabeth 173
Webb, Giles 116,133-135
Webb, John 1
Webb, Stephen 90
Webb, Thomas 173
Webb, William 8
Welby, Edward 77
Welch, William 157
Wells, John 109
Wentworth, Hugh 181
Werlbye, ----- 82
West, Capt. 28
West, Francis 22
West, Henry 36,131

NAME INDEX

PLACE INDEX

BRITISH ISLES

Bedfordshire
Milton Ernest 55
Berkshire
Sonning 52
Bristol
26,27,61,75,76,114,
115,134,153,162,176,
Swan Tavern 162
Cheshire
Worwall 99
Cornwall 166,173
Cambourne 167
Falmouth 40,147,75,77,
82,100,107,155,167
Fowey 167
Foy 179
Holford 3
Keivenhall 167
Lamorna Cove 167
Land's End 79
Lassick 147
Marazion 167
Millbrooke 26,179
Mousehole 167
Newland 167
Paul 167
Pendennis 36
Penzance 167
St. Cleeve 32
St. Ives 19,167,180
The Mount 167
Truro 147
Devon
Barnstaple 114,177
Bondreun 32
Brixton 68
Colliton 60
Dartmouth   20,28,107,
115,161,162,
165,177,178
Exeter 136,178

Devon (cont'd)
Ilfracombe 58
Kingswear 161
Limson 178
Madbury 82
Plymouth 3,19,22,37,
39,43,46,52,55,66,
68,69,99,100,105,109,
114,115,129,131,139,
145,161,165,166,168,
170,173,174,176,180
Salcombe 180
Stoke Fleming 162
Stoke Gabriel 3
Stonehouse 22
Sumford 176
Topsham 176,
Dorset
Dorchester 71
Langton 37
Poole 26,41
Weymouth 17,18,20,71,
77,82,84,85
Essex
Billericay 151
Chigwell 90
Colchester 63,79,178
Harwich 6,67-69,180
Lee 53,155
Leigh 123
Newland Fee 3
Stonedan Hall 82
Stratford by Bow 70
Tedingham 15
Tilbury 30,155
Walthamstow 013
Writtle 163
Gloucestershire
Tidnam 25
Winchcombe 14,15
Guernsey 25
Hampshire 135
Basingstoke 181

-211-

PLACE INDEX

PLACE INDEX

London & Middlesex
Staple Inn 13
Stepney 32,45,61,
62,93,96,106,107,
109,113,116,118,120
136-138,147,149,150
Thames St. 37,57,73
Three Cranes Tavern
56,93,96
Tower Hill 130,134,150
Tower Liberty/Precinct
41,119,131,132
Tower St. 41
Tower Wharf 65,176
Turnwheel Lane 58
Vintry 96
Wallbrook 41
Wapping 5,11-13,18-20
26,28,30,31,33,36,
40,43,45,47,48,54,
60,62,64,66,68,71,
72,77,78,80,81,87,91,
93,98,104,108,111,
114,116,118,119,122,
124,127,130,131,
137,140,142,145,
151,153,154,155,
158,159,166,171,
172,180,182
Wapping Wall 107
Whitechapel 20,50,79
100,135

Northumberland
Newcastle 121-123,143,
179

Norfolk
Noell 161
Norwich 136,137
Yarmouth 31,36,99,
134,135,178

Northants
Buckby 66
Grundan 66

Northants (cont'd)
Northampton 169
Oxfordshire
Grays near Henley 14
Oxford 181
Rollright 9
Scilly Isles
25,31,39,116,118,
128,141
Somerset
Ashton nr Bristol 115
Bedminster nr Bristol
115
Wilscombe 156
Staffordshire
Tunstall 41
Suffolk
Alborough 24
Ipswich 36,67-69,88,
91,100,105,116,
119,130,131
Needham 66
Orwell River 131
Southhold 145
Woodbridge 67,123
Surrey
Battersea 96
Bermondsey 78,85,94,
104
Burstow 53
Horsley Down 3,7,10,
33,71,83,165,180
Lambeth 181
Lambeth Marsh 60
Newington Butts 153
Redrith 6,10,14,25,
26,29,32-35,41,43,
44,60,62,71,83,86,
98,110,119,126,140,
141,143,154,161
Reigate 182
St. George, Southwark
38

PLACE INDEX

France (cont'd)
    Brest 147
    Brittany 35,36,141
    Burgundy 36
    Courtrai 163
    Dieppe 25,34,35,45
    Nantes 131,173
    Normandy 165
    Paris 34
    Picardy, 62
    Rochelle 14
    St. Malo 134
    St. Mure du Lossoi 36
    Ushant 141
Fyall 150,165
Guam 176
Hamburg 168
Holland 39,42,55,56,
            92-94,106,135,
            137,139,181
    Amsterdam 40,99,117,
            132,134,135,
            168,176,177
    Dunkirk 21,55
    Enchusen 161,167
    Flanders 133
    Flushing 16,58,59,94
    Madenblick 168
    Middleborough 133,134
    Ostend 67,158,165
    Oudtbeyrland 117
    Rotterdam 92-95,
            135-137
    Zealand 58,59,133,134

Italy
    Leghorn 4,5,170
    Marmora 177
    Messina 118
    Naples 97,118
    Ragusa 1
Persia 12
Portugal 162,177,180
    Faro 158,159
    Lisbon 114,118,159
    Oporto 112
Spain 91,113,158
    Azores 2
    Barcelona 53
    Bilbao 114,131,145,
                  173
    Cadiz 90,112,113,114,
                 169
    Canary Isles 169
    Cartagena 53
    Galicia 176
    Madeira 160,169
    Madrid 91
    Malaga 11,114,158,159
    Palma 149
    Seville 113
    St. Sebastian 131,168
Sweden
    Gothenburg 158